LEARNING
THE LANGUAGE OF REAL ESTATE

BARBARA COX, Ph.D.

SOUTH-WESTERN
THOMSON LEARNING

Australia · Canada · Mexico · Singapore · Spain · United Kingdom · United States

Learning the Language of Real Estate, 1st ed., by Barbara Cox

Executive Publisher: Dave Shaut
Senior Acquisitions Editor: Scott Person
Developmental Editor: Sara Froelicher
Production Editor: Amy McGuire
Marketing Manager: Mark Linton
Media Production Editor: Edward Stubenrauch
Manufacturing Coordinator: Charlene Taylor
Internal Design: Barbara Cox
Cover Design: Rik Moore
Cover Image: Photo Disc, Inc.
Production House: DPS Associates
Printer: Phoenix Color

Printed in the United States of America
1 2 3 4 5 04 03 02 01

For more information contact South-Western, 5101 Madison Road, Cincinnati, Ohio, 45227, or find us on the Internet at http://www.swcollege.com

For permission to use material from this text or product, contact us by
- **telephone: 1-800-730-2214**
- **fax: 1-800-730-2215**
- **web: http://www.thomsonrights.com**

Library of Congress Cataloging-in-Publication Data

Cox, Barbara G.,
    Learning the language of real estate / Barbara Cox.--1st ed.
        p. cm.
    Includes index.
    ISBN 0-324-14979-4
        1. Real estate business--Terminology. 2. Real property--Terminology. I. Title.

HD1365 .C688 2001
333.33'01'4--dc21   2001042649

CONTENTS

To the Users

Real estate professionals need an accurate understanding of a large number of terms from various disciplines. The worlds of law, architecture, finance, appraisal, and insurance contribute terms to the vocabulary that real estate agents, lenders, inspectors, and title and escrow professionals need to comprehend and use with precision.

Dictionaries are not always helpful. Real estate dictionaries and other reference books are usually written for professionals who already have some mastery of the profession rather than for learners. Textbooks, which should present helpful examples, aren't always clear or concise, and even the best of textbooks can be intimidating.

Learning the Language of Real Estate is intended to help prelicensees master the concepts and language used on licensing examinations and to help new agents and other professionals review and become more at ease with the terms they will be using throughout their career in real estate. Agents whose first language is not English or whose real estate background was formed outside the United States will find this book helpful and easy to understand. Instructors of real estate principles and other courses will find this book very useful for students who need extra practice with terminology.

This book has several features that will help ensure success in mastering the essential vocabulary of real estate. Before diving into the chapter that looks most interesting, look through the book and become familiar with these features.

- Each chapter presents a set of target words and phrases related to a particular aspect of real estate, such as ownership, appraisal, or escrow.

- Chapters are organized into sections, each with approximately three to eight terms. These short sections encourage learners to master the terminology a little at a time, and reduce the intimidation of learning such a large number of terms.

- Terms are defined in learner-friendly language.

- Plain-language, everyday examples help learners understand terms in the context of familiar, easy-to-remember situations.

Readers should think about these examples, called "Using Real Estate Terms," and try to think of similar situations from their own experience.

- "Use the Right Term" multiple choice questions follow each small section within a chapter, giving learners an immediate check on their understanding of the terminology in that section.

- Each chapter ends with several pages of multiple choice, true or false, fill-in, and short answer questions to help learners review all of that chapter's target words and phrases.

- The answers for the end-of-section and end-of-chapter questions are provided at the end of each chapter. The exception is the short answer questions, whose answers are found directly in the chapter definitions.

- An alphabetical list of terms at the beginning of each chapter gives learners a preview of the language included in that chapter. Learners should read the list carefully and ask themselves where they have heard the terms and if they are confident about their meanings.

- The terms for each section within a chapter are listed at the beginning of the section. These terms are given in the order in which they are presented in the section, which simplifies locating the information and understanding the organization of the section.

- Appendix I lists all the terms covered in the text according to chapter. The list will help learners review the terms and will help instructors plan discussions or develop additional material.

Learning the Language of Real Estate is indebted to Jerry Cox and David Silver-Westrick, co-authors of the *Prentice Hall Dictionary of Real Estate*, for applying their experience-based knowledge of real estate and clear thinking when reviewing the drafts. Alice Gilland provided unshakable faith in the project. Elizabeth Sugg asked her usual perspicacious questions at the time of the book's planning. Thank you all.

Chapter 1
DESCRIBING LAND

Where does your property end and the neighbor's property begin? How do you know? Where is this information kept on file? Terms related to these questions are addressed in this chapter. The six sections present the terms in the following groups: type of property; rectangular survey system; metes and bounds; assessor's descriptions; other land descriptions; and land or lot types.

Do You Know These Terms?

acre	meridian
air lot	metes and bounds
assessor's map	monument
base lines	personal property
bench mark	plat
chattel	principal meridian
contour map	quadrangle
corner lot	quarter section
cul de sac	range
fixture	raw land
flag lot	real estate, real property
front foot	relief map
government survey	section
guide meridian	single-loaded street
improvement	standard parallel
inside lot	T-lot
key lot	township
lot, block, tract	

1. Types of Property

real estate, real property	fixture
improvement	chattel
personal property	raw land

Know the difference between real property and personal property. In some instances, it's hard to tell!

real estate, real property

> land plus the improvements made to it and any rights to use the land and its improvements.

improvement

> something built on the land or affixed to it that is intended to be permanent. A house, church, warehouse, barn, fence, road, or landscaping is an example of an improvement.

personal property

> (also called *personalty*) things that are not part of the land or the improvement. Furniture, machinery, clothes, jewelry, and the like, are personal property. Personal property is usually transferred from one person or entity to another by means of a bill of sale. Personal property is not included in the transfer of real property.

fixture

> a part of the real estate, attached to the real estate, that was once personal property. For example, most furnaces, plumbing, ceiling lights, and doors are fixtures.

> Whether something is a fixture or not is important because fixtures are transferred as part of real property whereas personal property is not. The main test of whether something is a fixture is whether it was intended to become part of the real property when it was installed or attached.

> In commercial real estate, however, many fixtures remain personal property even though they may be attached. Display counters and heavy equipment, for example, may be bolted to the floor but remain personal property.

chattel

> a piece of personal property.

raw land

> land without any improvements; land in its natural state.

Using Real Estate Terms

George and Anita Barrow own a farm in the Midwest. The land and the farmhouse, barns, silo, fences, and the roads on the property taken as a whole are considered real property or real estate. All of those things except the land itself are considered improvements.

Examples of fixtures that are part of this property are the ceiling lights, barn hoists, milking dividers and machines attached in the barn, and ceiling fans.

The Barrows' farm machinery that is not a fixture, such as their tractors and bailers, as well as their furniture, antique kitchen stove, and animals are examples of personal property. Each of these is chattel.

Some of the Barrow farmland is dedicated to crops. This land is not considered raw land because it is not in its natural state. It has been cleared, prepared, sowed, irrigated, etc.

Across the highway from the Barrow farm is another piece of land the Barrows own. This land, however, has no improvements and is not being farmed. This land is in its natural state, and is considered raw land.

Use the Right Term

Circle the letter of the choice that best completes each statement. Use the definitions of the terms and your logic to determine the best answer. The answers are shown at the end of the chapter.

1. Kim Chang built a sturdy fence around his farm. The fence is _____.

   (a) personal property

   (b) an improvement

   (c) chattel

   (d) none of the above

2. Which of the following is not a fixture?

   (a) a built-in stove top

   (b) fancy kitchen sink faucet handles

   (c) an antique floor lamp

   (d) exterior window shutters

3. Which of the following is not real property?

   (a) Elizabeth Scott's residence

   (b) David Fitch's office building

   (c) John Meyer's empty lot

   (d) none of the above

4. Land plus the improvements made to it is _____.

   (a) personal property

   (b) real property

   (c) real and personal property

   (d) none of the above

5. An empty, unused lot is _____.

   (a) raw land

   (b) personal property

   (c) chattel

   (d) none of these

2. Rectangular Survey System

rectangular survey system
government survey
U. S. public land survey
meridian
principal meridian
guide meridian
base lines

standard parallel
quadrangle
range
section
township
acre

rectangular survey system, government survey, U. S. public land survey

a system established in 1785 as a way to describe land, particularly land in new U.S. territories and states. This system uses latitude and longitude lines to divide up the country. The land is further divided into quadrangles, ranges, townships, sections, and acres. The system is used to describe a great deal of land, but the recorded plat system (see the next section of this chapter) is used for more properties.

meridian, principal meridian

north-south longitude line. Some meridians were designated as principal meridians. The rectangular survey system has 36 principal meridians.

guide meridian

a meridian located 24 miles east and 24 miles west of a principal meridian. Guide meridians run between the standard parallels (see below).

base lines

latitude lines selected by the rectangular survey system as reference lines for the system. The rectangular survey system has 36 base lines.

standard parallel

a latitude line or parallel located 24 miles north and 24 miles south of a base line.

Figure 1.1   Parallels, Meridians, Base Line, Quadrangle

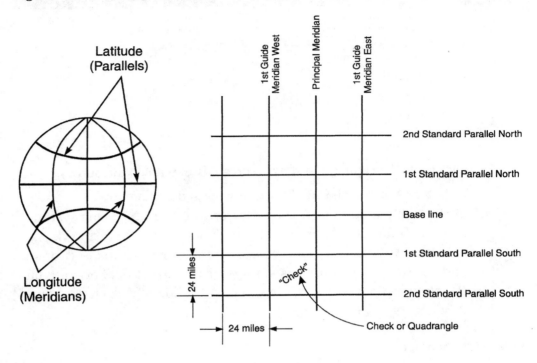

quadrangle

> (also called a *check*) a 24-mile-by-24-mile area created by guide meridians and standard parallels. A quadrangle is further divided into 16 equal six-mile-square areas. (See Figure 1.1.)

range

> a 6-mile-wide "column" defined by imaginary lines (longitudes) that are six miles to the east and six miles to the west of each principal meridian. Ranges are numbered consecutively as they go out from the principal meridian. The third range to the west of a principal meridian, for example, is named R3W, for Range, Third, West.

section

> a one-mile-square area that is an equal part of the 36 square miles of a township. Sections are numbered 1 through 36, beginning with the northeast corner and then running west, east, west (back and forth) along the townships. (See Figure 1.2.) A section contains 640 acres.

Partial sections are named according to their size and position in a section. A quarter section, for example is one fourth of a section. Its position is identified by compass names. The quarter section in the northeast corner of a section, for example, would be called the NE1/4.

Note: Because the earth curves, some sections may not be exactly 640 acres.

township

a strip of land six miles wide that runs east and west parallel to a baseline. The lines defining township strips (township lines) are drawn six miles north and six miles south of a base line. These township lines intersect with the range lines to create square areas that are six miles on each side (36 square miles) also called townships. The square area created by the intersection of range lines and township lines; 1/16 of a quadrangle, measuring six miles on each side.

Note: This use of the term *township* is not to be confused with the term that refers to political subdivisions.

Townships are numbered consecutively as they go out above or below the base line. For example, the strip (and all the township squares in it) that is the third township strip south of a base line is named T3S, for Township, Third, South.

acre

an area containing 43,560 square feet. There are 640 acres in a section.

Figure 1.2 Section, Townships (Figure source: *Principles of Real Estate*, 8th edition, by Charles J. Jacobus, page 24.)

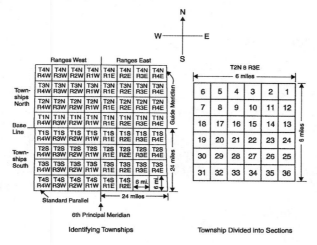

Use the Right Term

Circle the letter of the choice that best completes each statement. Use the definitions of the terms and your logic to determine the best answer. The answers are shown at the end of the chapter.

1. Meridians run _____ and base lines run _____.

   (a) sideways; up and down

   (b) north/south; east/west

   (c) east/west; north/south

   (d) none of the above

2. A standard parallel is parallel to a _____.

   (a) guide meridian

   (b) standard meridian

   (c) base line

   (d) longitude

3. A township _____.

   (a) has six sides

   (b) is six square miles

   (c) is six miles square

   (d) has sides one mile long

4. A section _____.

   (a) is an equal part of the 36 square miles of a township

   (b) contains 640 acres

   (c) is one square mile

   (d) all of the above

5. A 24-mile-by-24-mile area created by guide meridians and standard parallels is called a _____.

   (a) section

   (b) acre

   (c) quadrangle

   (d) township

3. Metes and Bounds

metes and bounds   bench mark
monument

metes and bounds

a system of describing land that uses specific points and angles and distances to describe the shape and boundaries of a parcel. *Metes* refers to measurements and directions; *bounds* refers to markers such as landmarks or monuments.

A metes and bounds description starts at a specifically identified starting point and moves from point to point around the parcel until it ends back at the starting point. The starting point is called the *point of commencement* or *point of beginning*.

Older metes and bounds descriptions identify a property by describing imaginary lines or physical ones that run from marker to marker. Other metes and bounds descriptions use directions shown as compass directions in degrees, minutes, and seconds of a circle. (See examples.)

monument

a landmark or marker named by a surveyor or a government that is used to set the boundary lines of a survey or property description. A monument may be natural, such as a river or mountain peak, or it could be something placed in a certain position and intended to be permanent, such as a stake or large stone.

In some instances, a corner in a section of the government survey system can be used as a monument. Although such a point is not necessarily marked with a visible marker, it can be accurately determined using the government survey system. (See the section on rectangular survey system.)

bench mark

permanent reference mark of known location and elevation, usually set into place by government surveyors. Surveyors use bench marks to measure elevations and altitudes above sea level for a surveyed area, as well as in their descriptions of the boundaries of a parcel.

An Old Parcel Description

Just for fun, have a look at this description prepared in 1721. You will appreciate our more recent methods of identifying or describing property!

... a certain tract or parcel of land called "Bennetts Adventure" lying and being on the North side of Wicocomoco Creek beginning at a marked pine dividing it from the land of Richard Stevens and from thence running East South East the breadth of 750 poles to a marked pine standing by Wicocomoco Bridge from thence running along upon the South side of a creek called by the Indians "Pattundicke" the length of 434 poles to a marked oak standing at the head of the aforesaid creek called "Pattundicke" from thence running West North West the breadth of 750 poles to a marked pine dividing it from the land of Richard Stevens with a line drawn South South West to the first bounder containing and laid out for 2500 acres more or less which said tract or parcel of land ... (Somerset Co. MD, Deed Book IK, p. 192.) ▲▲▲

Sample Metes and Bounds Description

Compare the drawing with the text below it, following the description from the permanent marker around the parcel.

Figure 1.3 Metes and Bounds

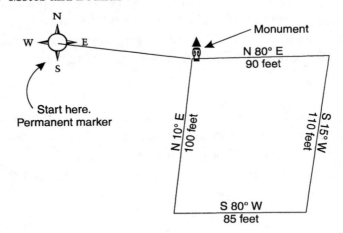

Beginning at the permanent marker, travel S65°E, 90' to the nearest corner of the parcel (where the monument is located), thence N80°E, 90'; thence S15°W, 110'; thence S80°W, 85'; thence N10°E, 100' back to the monument.

▲▲▲

Use the Right Term

Circle the letter of the choice that best completes each statement. Use the definitions of the terms and your logic to determine the best answer. The answers are shown at the end of the chapter.

1. A metes and bounds description _____.

    (a) uses monuments to identify specific locations

    (b) could use a river as part of its description

    (c) could use compass directions in degrees, minutes, and seconds of a circle

    (d) all of the above

2. A permanent reference mark of known location and elevation is _____.

    (a) a monument

    (b) a base line

    (c) a bench mark

    (d) a boundary line

3. A metes and bounds description starts at _____.

    (a) an angle

    (b) a point of commencement

    (c) a point of graduation

    (d) a specific distance

4. A monument could not be _____.

    (a) an old tree stump

    (b) a pile of stones

    (c) a parked truck

    (d) a creek

4. Assessor's Descriptions

lot, block, tract   assessor's map
plat

lot, block, tract

(also called *recorded map system* or *recorded survey system*) a
system of describing land that is based on a surveyor's map (plat)
filed in the public recorder's office.

plat

a map showing the location and boundaries of properties. A plat
shows the location and boundaries of the properties in a
subdivision, and is based on the surveyor's plat in the public
recorder's office. The subdivider gives each block in a tract a
number and gives each property a lot number. This map is then
placed in map books at the recorder's office.

assessor's map

a recorded map showing the parcel numbers assigned by the tax
assessor. The assessor's parcel number (APN) is used for tax
collection identification. APNs are also used by real estate
professionals and others to identify properties.

Assessors' maps are publicly available in the numbered pages of
numbered books for the various parts of a county. Each map has a
number and can be identified by book, page, and map number. The
maps for subdivided lots are usually based on the maps submitted
to the recorder's office by the subdivider at the time of subdivision.

Figure 1.4   Assessor's Map

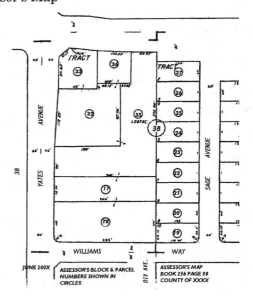

Use the Right Term

Circle the letter of the choice that best completes each statement. Use the definitions of the terms and your logic to determine the best answer. The answers are shown at the end of the chapter.

1. A plat is a _____.

    (a) plot of bare land

    (b) subdivided property

    (c) map

    (d) recorded deed

2. An assessor's map shows _____.

    (a) the assessor's number for each parcel

    (b) the assessor's number for each tract

    (c) the assessor's number for the county

    (d) only the subdividers lot number for each lot

3. Assessor's maps are _____.

    (a) publicly available

    (b) kept in numbered books in a state office

    (c) on numbered pages in file folders in locked cabinets

    (d) used only for subdivisions

4. A plat _____.

    (a) shows the location and boundaries of the properties in a subdivision

    (b) is based on the surveyor's plat in the public recorder's office

    (c) shows the subdivider's number for each block in a tract and a lot number for each property

    (d) all of these

5. Other Land Descriptions

contour map   air lot
relief map   front foot

contour map

(also called a *topographic map*) a map with contour lines that
indicate elevations. The contour lines connect points with the same
elevation.

Contour maps show slopes, hills, valleys, and other topographic
features. They indicate where land is level or where it must be
made level to create a buildable lot. See Figure 1.5.

Figure 1.5   Contour Map

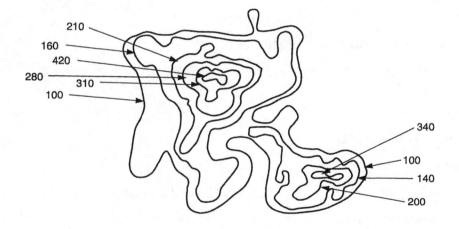

relief map

term used to describe a three-dimensional contour map.

air lot

space over a parcel of land. An air lot is defined by the parcel
description of the land and the elevation above the land.

front foot

one linear foot measured along the street side of a lot. Linear feet
are used as the basis for some assessment and valuation
calculations.

Use the Right Term

Circle the letter of the choice that best completes each statement. Use the definitions of the terms and your logic to determine the best answer. The answers are shown at the end of the chapter.

1. A measuring of a property's front footage indicates
   _____.

   (a) the distance across the front of the house

   (b) the number of feet around the perimeter of the property

   (c) the number of feet where the property meets the street

   (d) none of the above

2. A contour map shows _____.

   (a) the roofline of a house

   (b) a subdivider's lot numbers

   (c) hills and valleys

   (d) none of these

3. Erica Jamison wants to know if a particular area of the county is level.
   She needs a _____.

   (a) contour map

   (b) air map

   (c) surveyer

   (d) plat map

4. A contour map is also called a/an _____.

   (a) air map

   (b) topographic map

   (c) relief map

   (d) all of the above

6. Land or Lot Types

cul de sac   corner lot
flag lot   T-lot
key lot   single-loaded street
inside lot

cul de sac

a street that is open only at one end and that usually has a turn-around area at the closed end.

flag lot

a lot shaped like a flag with its flagpole. See Figure 1.6.

Using Real Estate Terms

To get to the Poulson's house, drive down the long driveway past the Curtis's house. The Poulson's house is behind the Curtis place. The long driveway is part of the Poulson's flag lot. (See Figure 1.6.) ▲▲▲

---

key lot

a lot adjoining the property line of a corner lot.

inside lot

a lot with a street on only one side.

corner lot

a lot that fronts on two or more streets. In many instances, a corner lot has somewhat higher value than an inside lot since it has greater access and sometimes more lighting.

T-lot

a lot that faces an incoming street at a T intersection.

single-loaded street

a street with houses situated along only one side. Single-loaded streets are often used on hillsides.

Figure 1.6 Lot Types

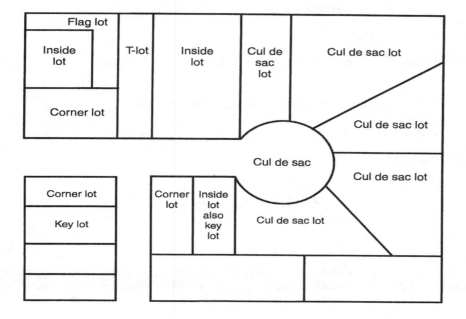

Use the Right Term

Circle the letter of the choice that best completes each statement. Use the definitions of the terms and your logic to determine the best answer. The answers are shown at the end of the chapter.

1. A street with houses situated along only one side is called a

    _____.

    (a) cul de sac

    (b) T street

    (c) single loaded street

    (d) one sided street

2. A lot with a street on only one side is _____.

    (a) a key lot

    (b) a flag lot

    (c) an inside lot

    (d) a single loaded lot

3. A T-lot is a _____.

    (a) lot shaped like a letter T

    (b) lot with a fence separating it from the next lot

    (c) lot with overdue Taxes

    (d) lot that faces an incoming street at a T intersection

4. A lot that fronts on two or more streets is called a _____.

    (a) double-sided lot

    (b) corner lot

    (c) T-lot

    (d) flag lot

Review & Practice: Describing Land

assessor's map	fixture
bench mark	improvement
contour map	quadrangle
corner lot	rectangular survey
cul de sac	standard parallel

Select the term from the list above that best fits the blank in each sentence below.

1. A _____ shows elevations of an area.

2. Jaime Rigas lives at the closed end of a block, near a circular turnaround area. Jaime lives on a _____.

3. An imaginary line that runs six miles north or six miles south of a base line and is parallel to the base line is called a _____.

4. Samuel Leach built a new barn at the back of his lot. The barn is a/an _____.

5. The permanent indoor hot tub that the Joneses installed last year is considered a/an _____.

6. The system that uses latitude and longitude lines to divide up and describe land is called the _____ system.

7. Intersecting guide meridians and standard parallels form a/an _____.

8. The _____ shows the number used by the county for property tax purposes.

9. A/An _____ is a permanent reference mark of known location and elevation.

10. A/An_____ has a street on at least two sides.

Short Answer

Use the space provided to answer the following questions.

1. What is the number of a township that lies in the second tier north of the base line and in the fourth tier east of the base line? Give both the tier and the range references.

2. Define and give an example of a *fixture*.

3. What is *real estate*? How does it differ from *personal property*?

4. How is an *assessor's map* different from a *recorded subdivider's plat*?

5. What is a *monument*?

Write the term that applies to each number in the figure below on the corresponding blank on page 21.

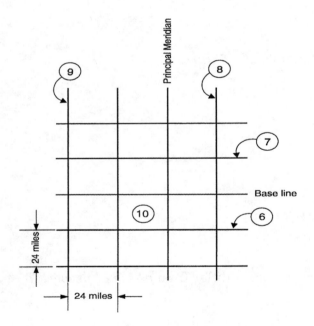

standard parallel south   standard parallel north
guide meridian east   guide meridian west
quadrangle

6. _____

7. _____

8. _____

9. _____

10. _____

True or False

Indicate whether each of the following statements is true or false by circling T or F. The answers are shown at the end of the chapter.

T F 1. A broken-down old barn is an improvement.

T F 2. An electrical outlet is personal property.

T F 3. An acre is a measure of area.

T F 4. A key lot is shaped like a key.

T F 5. A T-lot is shaped like a T.

T F 6. A flag lot is shaped like a flag with its flagpole.

T F 7. A contour map shows the slope of land.

T F 8. A single loaded street has homes on only one side.

T F 9. A plat is equal to one acre.

T F 10. A quarter section is equal to a quadrangle.

Answers

Types of Property: (1) b; (2) c; (3) d; (4) b; (5) a

Rectangular Survey System: (1) b; (2) c; (3) c; (4) d; (5) c

Metes and Bounds: (1) d; (2) c; (3) b; (4) c

Assessor's Descriptions: (1) c; (2) a; (3) a; (4) d

Other Land Descriptions: (1) c; (2) c; (3) a; (4) b

Land or Lot Types: (1) c; (2) c; (3) d; (4) b

Fill-In
(1) contour map; (2) cul de sac; (3) standard parallel; (4) improvement; (5) fixture; (6) rectangular survey; (7) quadrangle; (8) assessor's map; (9) benchmark; (10) corner lot

True or False
(1) T; (2) F; (3) T; (4) F; (5) F; (6) T; (7) T; (8) T; (9) F; (10) F

Much of the field of real estate is concerned with owners' rights and government or public rights. Who has the right to sell a property, or mortgage it, or rent it out? Who has the right to use it, for what purposes, and when? And who has a right to put a claim against a property, forcing its sale? This chapter addresses the terms we use to describe these various rights and restrictions.

This chapter is divided into six sections, addressing the following: freehold estate, leasehold estate, encumbrances (easements and encroachments), encumbrances (liens), power of the state, and other rights.

Do You Know These Terms?

air rights	freehold estate	mortgage lien
condemnation	general lien	periodic tenancy
dominant tenement	inverse condemnation	property tax lien
easement	involuntary lien	quiet enjoyment
easement appurtenant	judgment lien	remainder interest
easement by necessity	lease	remainderman
easement in gross	leasehold estate	reversionary interest
eminent domain	leasehold interest	reversioner
encroachment	lessee/lessor	right of way
encumbrance	lien	riparian rights
escheat	life estate	servient tenement
estate	life estate *pur autre vie*	specific lien
estate at will	life tenant	tenancy at sufferance
estate for years	littoral rights	voluntary lien
fee simple absolute	mechanic's lien	

The first two sections of this chapter address the two major categories of legal interest in real estate: *freehold estate* and *leasehold estate*. These two categories compare loosely to "own" and "rent." Figure 2.1 shows the types of interest within each of those two categorizations.

Figure 2.1 Estates					
Freehold Estate		Leasehold Estate			
Life Estate	Fee Simple Estate	Estate at Sufferance	Estate at Will	Estate for Years	Periodic Estate

1. Freehold Estates

freehold estate   reversionary interest
fee simple absolute   reversioner
life estate   remainder interest
life tenant   remainderman
life estate *pur autre vie*

freehold estate

one of the two major types of interest in land. Freehold estate implies ownership in the usual, non-technical meaning of the term. The other type of estate, leasehold estate, loosely means rental.

The two common types of freehold estate are *fee simple* (also called fee simple absolute) and *estate for life* (or life estate).

fee simple or fee simple absolute

the type of land ownership that gives the landowner the most rights possible. When land is owned this way, the owner and the owner's heirs own it forever. The owner can occupy and use the land, build on it, mortgage it, mine or drill on it, farm it, sell it or refuse to sell it, give it away, rent or lease it, or will it to heirs. Sometimes these rights are called the *fee simple bundle of rights*.

The rights that a landowner does *not* have are the rights that the government has—right of taxation, eminent domain, and escheat, for example. These terms are covered in a later section of this chapter.

life estate

> the type of freehold estate in which the owner holds a property only for his or her lifetime or for the lifetime of some other person.
>
> The person holding the property as a life estate is called the *life tenant*. If the term of the estate is measured by the lifetime of another person, the estate is called a *life estate pur autre vie* (for the life of another).
>
> Upon the death of the person who holds property as a life estate, the property either (a) goes back, or *reverts,* to the person who granted the life estate, called the *reversioner* (or to the estate of that person if deceased) or (b) goes to yet another person, who would be called the *remainderman*. Whether the property goes to a reversioner or a remainderman depends on the terms of the life estate. (See the following entries for further information.)
>
> The holder of a life estate may sell, give away, or will his or her interest to another. The terms of the original life estate will still apply.

Using Real Estate Terms

▶▶▶

Bill Fielding has decided to let his Aunt Lucy live in his house on Cedar Creek for the rest of her life. He grants her a life estate, which makes Aunt Lucy the life tenant.

▶▶▶

Frances Blanding decides that upon her death she would like her daughter to have her house. To make certain that her intentions are carried out, she decides to deed the house to her daughter now, but keep a life estate interest in the property. Frances has become the life tenant and can occupy the house for the rest of her life.

▶▶▶

Joan is going to inherit her brother's house. Until he dies, however, she needs a place to live. Joan's sister owns a small cottage, and she grants Joan a life estate in the cottage until their brother dies. In this example, the life estate is for the lifetime of the brother and is called a life estate *pur autre vie.* ▲▲▲

life tenant

> a person who possesses a life estate.

life estate *pur autre vie*

> a life estate whose duration is determined by the lifetime of someone other than the life tenant. (See example.)

reversionary interest

> the interest in a property held by a person (grantor) granting an interest in that property to another person with the provision that the property will return (revert) to the grantor upon a certain event or date. In a life estate, that event is the death of the life tenant or some other designated person.

reversioner

> the person holding the reversionary interest.

Using Real Estate Terms

Willard has granted his Aunt Nan a life estate interest in a house he owns on Elm Street, with the stipulation that when Aunt Nan dies, the house will revert back to Willard. In this case, Aunt Nan holds the life estate interest and Willard holds the reversionary interest. Aunt Nan is the life tenant and Willard is known as the reversioner. ▲▲▲

---

remainder interest, remainder estate

> an interest identical to reversionary interest except that the holder of a remainder interest is a third party, i.e., someone other than the grantor.

remainderman

> the person holding the remainder interest.

Using Real Estate Terms

Betsy, a widow who owns her own home, remarries. When Betsy prepares her will, she leaves ("bequeaths" or "devises") her home to her new husband *for his lifetime only.* (That is, the will creates a life estate.) She further stipulates that when this husband dies, the home will go to her son, Donald. The new husband will hold the property as a life estate. When he dies, the home goes to Donald. Donald is called the remainderman and is said to have remainder interest in the property. ▲▲▲

Use the Right Term

Circle the letter of the choice that best completes each statement. Use the definitions of the terms and your logic to determine the best answer. The answers are shown at the end of the chapter.

1. An advantage of holding a property as *fee simple absolute* is that
    _____.

    (a) the owner can sell the property

    (b) the owner can farm the property

    (c) the owner can will the property to his or her heirs

    (d) all of the above

2. Properties held as *freehold estates* _____.

    (a) can be life estates

    (b) are held free of debt

    (c) are leased

    (d) cannot be farmed

3. Eliza J. Colburn held a small property in Red Bank City. When she died, the property reverted to John Isaac Robins, who held reversionary interest in the property. Which of the following statements is true?

    (a) Eliza held the property as a leasehold estate.

    (b) Eliza held the property as a life estate.

    (c) John held the property as a life estate.

    (d) John was probably related to Eliza.

4. Using the example described in item 3, which of the following statements is true?

    (a) John held the property as a life estate.

    (b) John had granted Eliza the life estate interest in the Red Bank City property.

    (c) John held no interest in the property.

    (d) None of the above.

5. Miss Sarah Ward lives in a house in Marionville, which she holds as a life estate from the late Benjamin Custis. When Miss Sarah dies, according to Benjamin's will, the property will go to William Fitchett. Which of the following is true?

   (a) Benjamin Custis had leasehold interest in the Marionville house.

   (b) William Fitchett is the remainderman on the Marionville house.

   (c) Miss Sarah holds a reversionary interest on the property.

   (d) All of the above.

6. A person who receives interest in a property upon the death of the life tenant is _____.

   (a) the remainderman

   (b) the reversioner

   (c) the reversioner if he or she was the grantor of the life estate

   (d) greedy

7. A person who receives interest in a property upon the death of the life tenant is _____.

   (a) the remainderman

   (b) the reversioner

   (c) the remainderman if he or she was not the grantor of the life estate

   (d) breaking the law

8. Christopher Jones lives in a house in which he holds a life estate until his father dies. This arrangement is called _____.

   (a) a remainder estate

   (b) a reversionary estate

   (c) a life estate *pur autre vie*

   (d) an installment estate

2. Leasehold Estates

leasehold estate	lease
leasehold interest	lessee/lessor
estate at will	periodic tenancy
estate for years	tenancy at sufferance

leasehold estate, leasehold interest

an estate in land that includes possession but not ownership, as in leasing or renting. Types of leasehold estate include *estate at will*, *estate for years*, *periodic tenancy*, and *tenancy at sufferance*.

estate at will

a form of leasehold estate that the lessor or the lessee can terminate at any time.

estate for years

a form of leasehold estate (lease) with a specified beginning and ending. Although it uses the phrase "for years," the time does not necessarily need to be counted literally in years.

Using Real Estate Terms

Harriet Reason has a lease beginning on April 14, 2000, and ending on July 17, 2000. Even though this period is less than one year, it is an estate for years because it has a specified beginning and ending. ▸▸▸

---

lease

an agreement that gives someone the right to use a property for a period of time.

lessee/lessor

The person receiving permission to use the property according to a lease is called the *lessee* or *tenant*. The owner of the property is the *lessor* or *landlord*. Note also that the period of time is the *term*, and amount paid by the lessee for the use of the property is called the *consideration*.

periodic tenancy

(sometimes called *periodic estate*) a form of leasehold estate that includes automatic renewal until termination, as in a month-to-month lease.

tenancy at sufferance

> the tenancy established when a lessee continues to occupy a property beyond the legal time period and without express consent of the landlord.

Use the Right Term

Circle the letter of the choice that best completes each statement. Use the definitions of the terms and your logic to determine the best answer. The answers are shown at the end of the chapter.

1. Clara and William Downing are tenants in a house owned by David Scott. According to their agreement, the lease can be terminated at any time, either by the Downings or by the landlord. This arrangement is _____.

    (a) a tenancy at sufferance

    (b) an estate at will

    (c) periodic tenancy

    (d) illegal

2. Robert Willett rents an apartment from Parker Barnes. According to their agreement, the rental is "month-to-month," and either gentleman can terminate the agreement with 30 days notice. This arrangement is _____.

    (a) a tenancy at sufferance

    (b) an estate at will

    (c) periodic tenancy

    (d) an estate for years

3. George Corbin's lease expired nine days ago, but he continues to live in his leased cottage. Since the landlord has not given permission for George to remain on the property, George's occupancy of the property is _____.

    (a) a tenancy at sufferance

    (b) an estate at will

    (c) periodic tenancy

    (d) an estate for years

4. Ann Willis runs the Willis Dry Goods Store. She leases the store from her cousin Polly. Her current lease is for the period April 15 of this year through April 15 of next year. Ann's lease is _____.

(a) a tenancy at sufferance

(b) an estate at will

(c) periodic tenancy

(d) an estate for years

3. Encumbrances: Easements and Encroachments

encumbrance	easement in gross
easement	dominant tenement
easement appurtenant	servient tenement
easement by necessity	encroachment

encumbrance

> some type of claim against a property and an impediment to clear title. The main types of encumbrances are *easements*, *encroachments*, and *liens*. (Liens are treated in the next section.)

easement

> a right to use someone else's land for a special purpose. The owner of the land, however, does still own the land. Utility companies, such as telephone, water, and gas companies, commonly have easements on properties for such items as pipelines, poles, and power boxes.

> When a property is sold, an easement continues. Even through the land has a new owner, the easement is still part of the deal. In real estate language, this is usually stated as "an easement runs with the land."

> Two main categories of easements are *easements appurtenant* and *easements in gross*.

easement appurtenant

> an easement created for the benefit of a particular parcel of land, such as that granted to cross one property in order to reach another.

easement by necessity

an easement that allows a landowner to reach his or her "landlocked" parcel of land by crossing the land of another. An easement by necessity is a type of easement appurtenant.

easement in gross

an easement created for the benefit of a utility company or other entity; another parcel of land does not benefit from the easement.

dominant tenement

the property that benefits from an easement. In an *easement in gross,* there is no dominant tenement.

servient tenement

the property on which the easement is exercised; the property that "serves" another property or a utility.

encroachment

the presence of a wall, building, or other structure on another property without the property owner's permission.

Figure 2.2 Easements and Encroachments

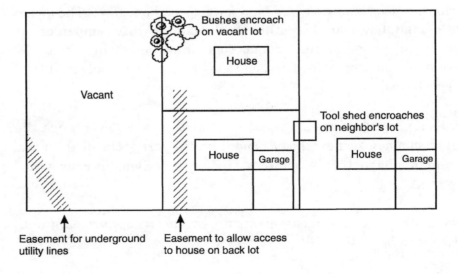

Use the Right Term

Circle the letter of the choice that best completes each statement. Use the definitions of the terms and your logic to determine the best answer. The answers are shown at the end of the chapter.

1. The only way that Edward Upshur can reach his house is to cross Thomas Savage's property. Edward Upshur's property is the _____.

    (a) servient tenement

    (b) dominant tenement

    (c) encroachment

    (d) life estate

2. Part of Oliver Stringer's tool shed is built on his neighbor's property. This is _____.

    (a) an encroachment on Oliver's property

    (b) an encroachment on the neighbor's property

    (c) an easement in gross

    (d) the right thing to do

3. Which of the following is an encroachment?

    (a) a gas meter on private property

    (b) a water pipe on public property

    (c) a wall built on a neighboring property

    (d) none of the above

4. In an easement in gross, _____.

    (a) there is no dominant tenement

    (b) there is no servient tenement

    (c) there are both dominant and servient tenements

    (d) there are no tenements

4. Encumbrances: Liens

lien	judgment lien
voluntary lien	mechanic's lien
involuntary lien	mortgage lien
specific lien	property tax lien
general lien	

lien

a form of encumbrance that is a claim against a property for money. Liens may be voluntary or involuntary, general or specific. Particular types of liens include *mechanic's liens, mortgage liens,* and *property tax liens.*

Liens, like other encumbrances, are impediments to title. Delinquent property taxes, which are liens, can result in a forced sale of the property to satisfy (pay) the lien. (Some other types of liens also have a "power of sale" and can force sale of the property to satisfy the lien.)

voluntary lien

a lien that a property owner has created. A mortgage lien is an example of a voluntary lien.

involuntary lien

a lien created by operation of a law, as in a property tax lien. Judgment liens and mechanic's liens are also involuntary liens.

specific lien

(also called *special lien*) a lien on a specific property. Compare this with general lien.

general lien

a lien on all the property of an owner within a given jurisdiction. A judgment lien, for example, is a lien on all the debtor's property in the county or counties where the judgment is filed. Federal and state taxes are also general liens.

judgment lien

a lien placed against the property, real and personal, of a debtor owing payment of money damages arising from a lawsuit.

Chapter 2: Land Rights & Interests

mechanic's lien

a lien against improvements or land resulting from nonpayment for labor or materials used for the improvement.

mortgage lien

a lien created when property is used by the owner as security for payment of a debt.

property tax lien

a lien placed on taxable property at the beginning of each tax year. This lien is removed when the property taxes have been paid. If the taxes are not paid, the government has the right to force the sale of the property to collect the unpaid tax.

Use the Right Term

Circle the letter of the choice that best completes each statement. Use the definitions of the terms and your logic to determine the best answer. The answers are shown at the end of the chapter.

1. John Trower built a small workshop for Wesley Tankard on Mr. Tankard's property in Exmore. Mr. Tankard failed to pay Mr. Trower for the work, so Mr. Trower filed a mechanic's lien. Which of the following is most likely to be true?

    (a) The lien is against all Mr. Tankard's properties, including the one in Exmore.

    (b) The lien is against the Exmore property only.

    (c) The lien is a general lien.

    (d) The lien is invalid because Mr. Tankard did not like the workshop Mr. Trower built.

2. A property tax _____.

    (a) is not a lien

    (b) is a voluntary lien

    (c) is a form of specific lien

    (d) is a form of general lien

3. A suit against Walter Jones results in a judgment lien against him.
    This judgment lien is a general lien, filed in three counties. Which of
    the following is true?

    (a) The lien is a voluntary lien.

    (b) Jones could lose only the properties in the county where the suit
        was filed and the judgment rendered.

    (c) All of Jones's properties in all three counties are at risk.

    (d) None of the above.

4. Which of the following is a true statement?

    (a) A property tax is a tax, not a lien.

    (b) A mortgage is a voluntary lien.

    (c) A mechanic's lien is a voluntary lien.

    (d) None of these.

5. Power of the State

eminent domain	inverse condemnation
condemnation	escheat

Government at various levels, national, states, and local, have rights or
powers related to the real estate of private citizens. The one we are most
familiar with is the power to tax.

Governments also have a power called *eminent domain,* which means the
state has a higher right than the property owner. The higher right is
related to the state's responsibility to care for the public good. If a
property is needed for a purpose that serves the public good, the
government has the power to take the property for its own use. When this
happens, the action is called *condemnation*, and the property owner is
paid a fair amount for it. The amount paid to the property owner is called
just compensation.

Other concepts related to governmental power and property are *inverse
condemnation* and *escheat.*

eminent domain

> the right of government, public utilities, and public service
> corporations to take private property for a necessary public use
> with just compensation paid to the owner.

Some entities with rights of eminent domain, in addition to state and federal governments, include school districts, sanitation districts, railroads, and power companies.

condemnation

the taking of private property for public good. Property owners whose property is condemned are entitled to be paid just compensation for the property.

Using Real Estate Terms

The town of Rivercity needed to widen a street to make it safe for public use. Widening the street required using a piece of land owned by Rebecca Montrose. The town government, exercising its right of eminent domain, condemned Rebecca's property, paying her a fair amount for it. Rebecca did not wish to sell or otherwise lose or transfer her property, but the town government's right to use the property for public good was greater than Rebecca's right to it. ▲▲▲

---

inverse condemnation

an action to seek compensation from the state begun by an owner whose property has been taken without condemnation and accompanying compensation.

escheat

the taking of a property by the state when the owner dies without a will or heir.

Using Real Estate Terms

Larry Hope never made a will and had no children or other identifiable heirs. When Larry died, the state took his property, sold it, and kept the proceeds. The property was taken by escheat. ▲▲▲

Use the Right Term

Circle the letter of the choice that best completes each statement. Use the definitions of the terms and your logic to determine the best answer. The answers are shown at the end of the chapter.

1. When the county condemned Sarah Whitehead's property, _____.

   (a) it was committing an illegal act

   (b) it was exercising its right of eminent domain

   (c) it was escheating the owner

   (d) none of the above

2. When the county constructed a sewage treatment plant, the foul odor carried downwind to Rudy Dolby's house. Rudy's house lost value, because Rudy could not sell it for the amount it would have brought before the plant. Rudy filed to get the county to condemn his property and pay him just compensation. This action is called _____.

   (a) eminent domain

   (b) condemnation

   (c) inverse condemnation

   (d) escheat

3. James Dix died without a will and without offspring or other heirs. The state took his property. This action is called _____.

   (a) eminent domain

   (b) escheat

   (c) condemnation

   (d) inverse condemnation

4. William and Ann Marshall owned property near a highway. When the state decided to build an on-ramp, it condemned the Marshalls' property. Which of the following is true?

   (a) The state had the right to do this.

   (b) The state used its right of eminent domain.

   (c) The state had to pay the Marshalls just compensation for their property.

   (d) All of the above.

6. Other Rights

air rights

littoral rights

quiet enjoyment

right of way

riparian rights

Other rights related to property include air rights, littoral rights, quiet enjoyment, right of way, and riparian rights. Some of these rights may be sold.

air rights

the right to use the space above a property. Air rights may be sold or leased for airplanes, satellite dishes, or bridges. When the property is sold, certain agreements about the air rights go along with the sale.

littoral rights

a landowner's right to use the water of a sea or ocean bordering his or her land. Littoral land is that which borders on the sea or ocean.

quiet enjoyment

the right to possess and use one's property without undue disturbance from others.

right of way

a right to cross a specified portion of another person's property.

riparian rights

a landowner's right to use the water of a river or stream bordering his or her land.

Use the Right Term

Circle the letter of the choice that best completes each statement. Use the definitions of the terms and your logic to determine the best answer. The answers are shown at the end of the chapter.

1. When airplanes flew too low over Adam's house, he complained that the airlines were violating his _____.

   (a) air rights

   (b) ear rights

   (c) riparian rights

   (d) none of the above

2. The Parkers complained to local authorities that the noise from a new 24-hour skateboard center was disrupting their sleep. They claimed that the center was violating their _____.

   (a) air rights

   (b) right of way

   (c) right to quiet enjoyment

   (d) littoral rights

3. Farmer Crockett used the water from a stream that bordered his property to irrigate his fields. The rights he was exercising were his _____ rights.

   (a) littoral

   (b) agrarian

   (c) watering

   (d) riparian

4. Leah Holland gave her cousin permission to drive across the back of her property to reach town more quickly. This meant that her cousin had _____.

   (a) an encroachment

   (b) a right of way

   (c) littoral rights

   (d) a leasehold estate

Review & Practice: Land Rights and Interests

servient tenement	estate for years
easement in gross	periodic tenancy
eminent domain	property tax lien
escheat	quiet enjoyment
estate at will	voluntary lien

Select the term from the list above that best fits the blank in each sentence below.

1. A _____ is the type of freehold estate in which the owner holds a property for his or her lifetime only.

2. Henry Pigott died without legal heirs and without a will. The state took his property. This is known as _____.

3. A form of leasehold estate that the lessor or the lessee can terminate at any time is called _____.

4. Jane and Mark rent their apartment on a month-to-month basis. Their tenancy is called _____ .

5. An easement created for a utility company's cables is called a/an

    _____.

6. Thomas Evans has an easement on William Joyner's property to reach his house from the street. William Joyner's property is the _____ tenement.

7. An example of an involuntary lien is _____.

8. The power of the government to condemn private property is known as _____.

9. A mortgage is an example of _____ .

10. An owner's right to use his or her property without undue disturbance is known as _____.

Short Answer

Use the space provided to answer the following questions.

1. What is the difference between a *freehold estate* and a *leasehold estate*?

2. Define and give an example of *reversionary interest*.

3. Define and give an example of *remainder interest*.

4. Explain the difference between an *easement in gross* and an *easement appurtenant*.

5. Under what conditions does an *escheat* occur?

6. Explain the difference between a *specific lien* and a *general lien*.

7. List four types of *leasehold estates*.

8. A sound and well-maintained property may be "condemned" by the state. Explain.

9. Explain the difference between a *lessee* and a *lessor*.

10. A mortgage lien is an example of a voluntary lien; a property tax lien is an example of an involuntary lien. Explain the difference between a *voluntary lien* and an *involuntary lien*.

True or False

Indicate whether each of the following statements is true or false by circling T or F. The answers are shown at the end of the chapter.

T F 1. The type of land ownership that gives the owner the most rights is called fee simple absolute.

T F 2. A life estate is a form of lease.

T F 3. Periodic tenancy refers to occupying a property only occasionally.

T F 4. An easement that allows access to a landlocked property is called an easement by necessity.

T F 5. The presence of a wall, building, or other structure on a neighboring property without permission is called an encumbrance.

T F 6. Permission to use a part of someone's property for a special purpose is called eminent domain.

T F 7. Liens may be voluntary or involuntary.

T F 8. A general lien is always voluntary.

T F 9. Riparian refers to rivers and streams, whereas littoral refers to seas or oceans.

T F 10. Property owners whose property is condemned are entitled to be paid just compensation for the property.

Answers

Freehold Estates: (1) d; (2) c; (3) b; (4) b; (5) b; (6) c; (7) c; (8) c

Leasehold Estates: (1) b; (2) c; (3) a; (4) d

Encumbrances—Easements and Encroachments: (1) b; (2) b; (3) c; (4) a

Encumbrances—Liens: (1) b; (2) c; (3) c; (4) b

Power of the State: (1) b: (2) c; (3) b; (4) d

Other Rights: (1) a; (2) c; (3) d; (4) b

Fill-In
(1) life estate; (2) escheat; (3) an estate at will; (4) periodic tenancy; (5) easement in gross; (6) servient; (7) a property tax lien; (8) eminent domain; (9) a voluntary lien; (10) quiet enjoyment

True or False
(1) T; (2) F; (3) F; (4) T; (5) F; (6) F; (7) T; (8) F; (9) T; (10) T

Chapter 3
OWNERSHIP

Rights of property owners may depend on whether they own the land alone or together with other people. What are these rights? The most important ones are related to the right to sell or give away the property or the owner's "interest in" the property or to mortgage the property (that is, use it as collateral for a loan).

What are different ways that people can own property? In what ways can they share ownership, or "interest" in, a property? This chapter explores the types of property ownership and rights that go along with them.

Do You Know These Terms?

community property	tenancy for life; life estate
concurrent ownership	tenancy in common
estate in severalty	undivided interest
joint tenancy	unities
partition	unity of interest
right of survivorship	unity of possession
separate property	unity of time
sole ownership	unity of title
tenancy by the entirety	

1. One Owner Only, Please

The terms we use to describe ownership of a property by just one person or entity include the following:

estate in severalty	sole ownership
separate property	

estate in severalty

sole ownership. In this case, the word *severalty* is an old word that means "separately." We use it to distinguish from *jointly*. Think of severalty as the opposite of jointly.

separate property

a special case of sole ownership. Sometimes referred to as *sole and separate property*, this term refers to property that was owned prior to marriage in a community property state. (See community property in the next section.) Property that is purchased with separate funds or acquired by gift or inheritance after marriage can also be exempted from (not included in) a couple's community property and considered to be separate property. Separate property can be conveyed (sold or given) or mortgaged without the signature or other permission of the owner's spouse.

Using Real Estate Terms

Charles Meyers' wife, Edith Meyers, inherited a small house from her Aunt Frances. The house was inherited as Edith's separate property. Although Charles was not in favor of selling the little house, Edith had the right to do so without his permission or signature. ▲▲▲

sole ownership

> ownership of a property by only one person or entity. The owner could be a person or a business or a trust, but the property is only owned by one owner.

Use the Right Term

Circle the letter of the choice that best completes each statement. Use the definitions of the terms and your logic to determine the best answer. The answers are shown at the end of the chapter.

1. An advantage of sole ownership for a person is that _____.

    (a) the owner can make all the decisions about the property

    (b) the owner's spouse shares responsibility for property maintenance

    (c) the owner can make the mortgage payments early

    (d) all of the above

2. Properties held as estates in severalty _____.

    (a) have had several owners in the past

    (b) have been subdivided

    (c) are held separately by one owner

    (d) consist of three or more parcels of land

3. Separate property _____.

    (a) can be sold without approval of the owner's spouse

    (b) refers to property held prior to the owner's marriage

    (c) can refer to property inherited by a married person

    (d) all of the above

2. Two Owners or More

Ownership of a property by two or more persons or other entities at the same time ("concurrent" or occurring together) is considered *concurrent ownership*. Three common forms of concurrent ownership are *community property*, *joint tenancy*, and *tenancy in common*. *Tenancy by the entirety* is a special form of joint ownership for married persons.

community property   tenancy by the entirety
joint tenancy   tenancy in common

community property

a form of property ownership in marriage in some states, including Arizona, California, Idaho, Louisiana, Nevada, New Mexico, Texas, and Washington. Community property is all property not owned by a husband or wife prior to the marriage or acquired during the marriage by gift or inheritance, and which is deemed to be the fruit of the efforts of both parties. Both parties are entitled to a one-half share of all such real and personal property, which each party may sell, devise, or will.

The rights associated with community property do not generally include a *right of survivorship* (see entry for joint tenancy). However, as of July 1, 2001, California allows title to be held as community property with this right.

joint tenancy

one of several forms of shared ownership in which more than one person owns an interest in the same real property. The traditional test for joint tenancy is the application of the *Four Unities*. (1) *Unity of title*—all owners share one title; (2) *Unity of time*—the joint tenancy must be created by grant or will, executed and delivered at one time; (3) *Unity of interest*—each joint tenant must have an equal interest in the property; (4) *Unity of possession*—each owner must have an equal right to possess and enjoy the entire property.

Joint tenancy includes a *right of survivorship,* meaning that, if one joint tenant dies, the surviving joint tenant(s) automatically receive the decedent's interest or "share" as a matter of law. If a joint tenant sells or grants his or her interest to another, the new owner holds title as a *tenant in common* with the remaining joint tenants.

Using Real Estate Terms

The large house on Andover Creek was owned by four Potter cousins by joint tenancy. By unity of interest they share in the property equally, each with a one-fourth share. When one cousin, Amy Potter, dies, the other three cousins will receive Amy's share, according to the right of survivorship that is a part of joint tenancy. The three cousins will then each own a one-third share in the property. ▲▲▲

tenancy by the entirety

an estate created by the conveyance to a husband and wife with the right of survivorship. Upon the death of either the husband or the wife, the title to the whole property passes to the survivor to the exclusion of the deceased's other heirs. The termination of this estate requires the joint action of both husband and wife. Compare with *joint tenancy,* which may be broken by the conveyance of an interest by either the husband or wife. States usually do not recognize both tenancy by the entirety and joint tenancy.

Using Real Estate Terms

Jacob and Hilda Brandt own their home as tenancy by the entirety. Neither Jacob nor Hilda alone can sell, give away, or otherwise transfer the property. According to tenancy by the entirety, they must take such an action together. When either Jacob or Hilda dies, the survivor will have title.

Jacob has three adult children by a prior marriage. Even so, if Jacob were to die before Hilda, those children would not receive any interest in the property. ▲▲▲

---

tenancy in common

a form of shared (concurrent) ownership recognizing concurrent possession by more than one person with each having an undivided interest in the entire estate. Unlike joint tenancy, tenancy in common may be established by separate instruments. No co-tenant can exclude the other co-tenants from any portion of the property or partition possession to the property.

In tenancy in common, the shares may be unequal, and the co-tenant may sell or will his share without disturbing the co-tenancy relationship. Each co-tenant bears his proportional share of maintaining the property, and is entitled to a proportionate share of the income from the property. There is no right of survivorship.

Using Real Estate Terms

The apartment complex at 406 Main Street was owned by Ann Hunt, Brian Trower, and Carlos Evans as tenants in common. Ann Hunt owned a 50 percent share, Brian Trower owned a 30 percent share, and Carlos Evans owned a 20 percent share. As allowed by tenants in common principles, Carlos Evans sold his share in the property to Danielle Skipper. Now Danielle Skipper is the third co-tenant; she has the 20 percent share.

Ann Hunt pays 50 percent of the maintenance and taxes and any other expenses related to the property. She also receives 50 percent of the rents. Likewise, Carlos and Danielle pay their share of expenses and receive their share of the rents (30 and 20 percent, respectively). ▲▲▲

Use the Right Term

Circle the letter of the choice that best completes each statement. Use the definitions of the terms and your logic to determine the best answer. The answers are shown at the end of the chapter.

1. In tenancy by entirety, upon the death of either the husband or the wife, _____.

    (a) the title to the whole property passes to the survivor to the exclusion of the deceased's other heirs

    (b) the entire property passes to the direct descendants of the deceased

    (c) the state takes the property

    (d) none of these

2. Mr. and Mrs. Joynes live in a community property state. Before they were married, Mr. Joynes gave his bride-to-be a cottage by a lake. The cottage is _____.

    (a) community property

    (b) Mr. Joynes's property, held concurrently with Mrs. Joynes

    (c) Mrs. Joynes's sole property

    (d) none of these

3. The Burton Building is owned by the three Burton brothers as a tenancy in common. This income from the property is

   _____.

   (a) shared equally by the three brothers

   (b) divided among the three brothers in proportion to the size of each brother's share of the building

   (c) paid to a fourth party who manages the building for the Burtons

   (d) equal to the expenses of maintaining the building

4. The Nottinghams bought and own a property in joint tenancy. Each of them _____.

   (a) owns the part of the property that he or she paid for

   (b) has an equal right to enjoy the entire property

   (c) has a right to enjoy his or her part of the property

   (d) can sell or give his or her part only to one of the others

3. Unities

unities	unity of time
unity of interest	unity of title
unity of possession	

unities

the legally required characteristics of joint tenancy. In essence, the joint tenants must take title to the property at the same time, and by the same instrument. They must have the same title (all joint tenants), and must each enjoy an undivided right of possession and enjoyment. A failure of one or more of these conditions will usually result in the creation of a tenancy in common.

unity of interest

a required element of a joint tenancy. Interests in the real property must accrue by the same conveyance. In other words, a joint tenancy cannot be created through a series of conveyances in which individual joint tenants are added.

unity of possession

> a required element of a joint tenancy. Each joint tenant must enjoy an undivided right to possess and enjoy the entire property. No tenant can claim a specific part of the property as his own to the exclusion of the other joint tenants.

unity of time

> a required element of a joint tenancy. All joint tenants must take title at the same time.

unity of title

> a required element of a joint tenancy. All joint tenants must hold the same title to the property. (By contrast, in a tenancy in common, the tenants may have ownership by several titles.)

True or False

Indicate whether each of the following statements is true or false by circling the T or the F. The answers are shown at the end of the chapter.

T F   1. Joint tenants can add more joint tenants at a later time.

T F   2. The four unities are time, possession, title, and estate.

T F   3. In unity of possession, each joint tenant has one particular part of the property "unified" under his or her own control.

T F   4. The four unities are all requirements of joint tenancy and tenancy in common.

T F   5. Unity of time means that the owners must be present at the property at the same time.

T F   6. If three of the four unities are true, but the fourth one is not, a tenancy in common, rather than joint tenancy, usually results.

4. Related Terms

Several terms related to ownership describe specific rights or actions. Four such terms that are important to know are:

partition	right of survivorship
tenancy for life	undivided interest

partition

a court order separating multiple ownership interests, usually to allow an owner to sell or otherwise convey his or her interest when the other owners do not wish to convey their interests.

tenancy for life; life estate

an ownership interest in real property that has a duration measured by the life of the grantee of the life estate, (a life tenant), or the life of another person (tenancy *pur autre vie*). At the death of the life tenant (the person granted the ownership interest) or at the death of the person whose life serves as the limitation of the estate, the estate passes either to the *reversioner* (the person who granted the estate), or the *remainderman* (another person named by the grantor of the estate).

right of survivorship

a unique characteristic of a *joint tenancy* that gives the surviving tenant (owner) the interest previously held by the deceased joint tenant without need for or requirement of probate proceedings. In other words, title passes automatically upon the death of one joint tenant to the other(s).

undivided interest

the interest a co-owner has in a parcel of real property. The interest is a fractional interest in the whole property, not a 100 percent interest in a portion of the property. Tenants in common and joint tenants hold undivided interest.

Use the Right Term

Circle the letter of the choice that best completes each statement. Use the definitions of the terms and your logic to determine the best answer. The answers are shown at the end of the chapter.

1. Edgar Fitch, George Harmonson, and Julia, daughter of George and wife of Edgar, together own a residence in a non-community-property state. They hold title as tenants in common. Which of the following statements is *known* to be true?

   (a) Julia will inherit her father's share.

   (b) Each person owns an undivided interest of one-third of the whole property.

    (c) George has tenancy for life.

    (d) Each person owns an undivided interest of some percentage of the whole property.

2. George passes away. What happens?

    (a) Edgar and Julia have right of survivorship and automatically receive George's share, half each.

    (b) Edgar and Julia do not have right of survivorship and do not automatically receive any of George's share.

    (c) Edgar and Julia sue George's estate to obtain their right of survivorship.

    (d) None of these.

3. Julia decides to give her share to her daughter, Sarah. Edgar and George don't want her to. What does Julia do?

    (a) Asks the court to partition her share so she can give it to Sarah.

    (b) Nothing. As a tenant in common, Julia cannot give any part of her share to anyone else.

    (c) She gets permission from Edgar and then writes up a letter declaring the gift.

    (d) None of these.

4. As it turns out, Edgar's interest in the property is a tenancy for life. George had given him that interest when Edgar and Julia got married. George named Julia as the remainderman, which means that when Edgar dies, Julia will have his interest in the property. Which of the following statements is true?

    (a) This description is not possible because they hold the property as tenants in common so Edgar cannot have tenancy for life interest.

    (b) George cannot name Julia as the remainderman.

    (c) The description could be accurate.

    (d) None of these.

Review & Practice: Ownership

estate in severalty	tenant(s) in common
joint tenancy	undivided interest
right of survivorship	unities
separate property	unity of interest
tenancy for life	unity of time

Select the term from the list above that best fits the blank in each sentence below.

1. _____ can be conveyed (sold or given) or mortgaged without the signature or other permission of the owner's spouse.

2. Sometimes sole ownership is called_____.

3. According to_____, each joint tenant must have an equal interest in the property.

4. By _____, title passes automatically upon the death of one joint tenant to the other(s).

5. If a joint tenant sells or grants his or her interest to another, the new owner holds title as a_____ with the remaining joint tenants.

6. _____are the legally required characteristics of joint tenancy.

7. In _____, the owners must take title to the property at the same time, and by the same instrument.

8. According to_____, all joint tenants must take title at the same time.

9. _____is a fractional interest in the whole property, not a 100 percent interest in a portion of the property.

10. An ownership interest in real property that has a duration measured by the life of the grantee of the life estate or the life of another person is called _____.

Short Answer

Use the space provided to answer the following questions.

1. List the *four unities* and define each.

2. Define *estate for life*. Give an example.

3. Define *community property*. Give an example.

4. List eight community property states.

5. What is *right of survivorship*? Give an example.

6. Describe *tenancy in common*. Give an example.

7. What is a *life estate*?

8. What is the difference between a *reversioner* and a *remainderman*?

9. Tenants in common, joint tenants, and holders of community property hold an undivided interest in the subject property. Explain.

10. What is accomplished by a court order called a partition?

True or False

Indicate whether each of the following statements is true or false by circling T or F. The answers are shown at the end of the chapter.

T F 1. Separate property refers to a house that is detached from other houses, i.e., a house that is not a condominium.

T F 2. In tenancy in common, the shares may be unequal, and the co-tenant may sell or will his share without disturbing the co-tenancy relationship.

T F   3. Tenancy by the entirety is a special form of joint ownership for married persons.

T F   4. Separate property can refer to property that was owned prior to marriage in a community property state.

T F   5. Unity of possession is required of tenancy in common but not of joint tenancy.

T F   6. According to right of survivorship, a person's children are always heir to his or her property.

T F   7. A court order called a partition requires the co-owners to put up walls or dividers to demarcate which part of the property belongs to each co-owner.

T F   8. Undivided interest is another term for sole ownership.

T F   9. Tenancy in common and community property are equivalent terms.

T F 10. In tenancy in common, no co-tenant (co-owner) can exclude the other co-tenants from any part of the property.

Answers

One Owner Only, Please: (1) a; (2) c; (3) d

Two Owners or More: (1) a; (2) c; (3) b; (4) c

Unities: (1) F; (2) F: (3) F; (4) F; (5) F; (6) T

Related Terms: (1) d; (2) b; (3) a; (4) c

Fill-In
(1) separate property; (2) estate in severalty; (3) unity of interest; (4) right of survivorship; (5) tenant in common; (6) unities; (7) joint tenancy; (8) unity of time; (9) undivided interest; (10) tenancy for life

True or False
(1) F; (2) T; (3) T; (4) T; (5) F; (6) F; (7) F; (8) F; (9) F; (10) T

Chapter 4
TRANSFER OF OWNERSHIP

Ownership of property can change. An owner might sell a property to another party. Property might be inherited by a spouse, children, or other heirs when the owner dies. Or the ownership of a property might be forfeited or lost.

The first two sections of this chapter deal with terms related to the transfer of ownership by virtue of sale or gift—in other words, a voluntary transfer of ownership by a living owner. The third section presents terms related to the transfer of ownership after the death of the owner. The fourth section addresses othe r forms of ownership transfer, mostly involuntary or beyond the control of the owner.

Do You Know These Terms?

accession	covenants and	guardian deed
accretion	warranties	holographic will
administrator/	decedent	intestate
administratrix	dedication	land patent
adverse possession	deed	legacy, legatee
alienation of title	devise, devisee	nuncupative or oral will
alluvion	executor/executrix	probate
avulsion	executor's deed	quitclaim deed
bargain and sale deed	forfeiture of title	reliction
bequeath, bequest	gift deed	Statute of Frauds
codicil	grant	testate
consideration	grant deed	testator/testatrix
convey, conveyance	grantee	warranty deed
correction deed	grantor	will

---

1. Deeds

convey, conveyance	consideration
deed	covenants and warranties
grant	grant deed
grantee	warranty deed
grantor	Statute of Frauds

How is property transferred, or "conveyed," from one owner to another? Usually by means of a *deed*. This section includes terms related to the terms and actions required to create a deed, as well as a comparison of the two main types of deed: *grant deed* and *warranty deed*.

convey, conveyance

> to transfer. In real estate, the term is usually used in the phrase "convey title" or "convey ownership." The noun form, conveyance, refers to (a) the act of conveying and (b) the document that is used to transfer the ownership, usually a deed.

Using Real Estate Terms

When Kevin Chang died, according to the terms of his will, his Hill Street property was conveyed to Marcella Jones. ▲▲▲

deed

the legal document that conveys ownership of property from one person or entity to another. A deed must be written and it must identify (a) the grantee and grantor; (b) the consideration; and (c) the property according to a legal description. The deed must contain words of conveyance, that is, words that transfer the ownership. Also, to be valid, a deed must be signed by the grantor. Furthermore, most deeds show the date of the deed and a sworn acknowledgement that the grantor is transferring the property of his or her own free will.

The most common form of deed is a *warranty deed*. However, some states, including California, Idaho, and North Dakota, use a *grant deed*.

grant

to give; to transfer ownership from the present owner, the *grantor*, to the new owner, the *grantee*.

grantee

the party acquiring the property. This could be a buyer, a person receiving the property as a gift or as an inheritance, or some other person or entity acquiring the property.

grantor

the party transferring ownership; the present owner.

Using Real Estate Terms

Jane Robins sold her mountain cabin to Eve and Ed Moser. On the deed, Jane Robins is the grantor and the Mosers are the grantees. ▲▲▲

---

consideration

something given in exchange for something else. A deed must specify that the property is being transferred in exchange for something of value, the consideration or "valuable consideration." The consideration could be an amount of money, services, or, in the case of a gift, natural love and affection.

covenants and warranties

promises made by a grantor, especially promises that the title to the property being conveyed is clear (good; valid). Warranties include a penalty or form of compensation to be paid by the grantor in the event that the promised act is not performed.

The five most common covenants are:

(a) **Covenant against Encumbrances**, which promises that the property is clear of encumbrances other than any that might be specifically listed in the deed;

(b) **Covenant of Further Assurance**, which promises that the grantor will do whatever is necessary to transfer the title to the grantee;

(c) **Covenant of Quiet Enjoyment**, which promises that the grantee will have the property free of claims by others;

(d) **Covenant of Seisin**, in which the grantor promises that he or she owns the property, is in possession of it, and has the right to sell it; and

(e) **Covenant of Warranty of Title**, which promises that the grantor will pay for defending the grantee's rights to the property in the event that some third party should ever assert a rightful claim to the property.

(See Figure 4.1.)

grant deed

a deed used in some states, including California, Idaho, and North Dakota. A grant deed uses fewer covenants and warranties than a warranty deed. The grant deed includes covenants and warrants by the grantor that he or she has not previously transferred the property to someone else, has not encumbered the property except as specifically stated in the deed, and that, in the event of acquiring some title to the property in the future, he or she will convey that title to the grantee.

warranty deed

(sometimes called a *general* warranty deed or a *full covenant* and warranty deed) a deed used in most states and that is generally considered to have the most warranties to protect the grantee. A warranty deed includes all five of the covenants listed in the entry for *covenants and warranties* given above.

Statute of Frauds

the statute requiring conveyance of real estate to be in writing and to be signed by the grantor.

Figure 4.1 Warranty Deed

Warranty Deed

This deed is made this _____17th_____ day of ___January, 20XX___,
in the city of ___River Bend___, state of ___AA___, between
Cedric Neal_____ , residing at ___618 Seabright Street, River
Bend, AA_____ , hereinafter called the Grantor, and ___Robert and
Joanna Silver, husband and wife as joint tenants___ located at
60482 Market Avenue, River Bend, AA_____ , hereinafter called the
Grantee.

Witness that in consideration of one hundred dollars ($100.00) and other
valuable consideration paid by the Grantee to the Grantor, the Grantor does
hereby grant and convey unto the Grantee, the Grantee's heirs and assigns
forever, the following described parcel of land:

[legal description of property inserted here]

together with the buildings and improvements thereon and all the estate and
rights pertaining thereto, to have and to hold the premises herein granted unto
the Grantee, the Grantee's heirs and assigns forever.

The premises are free from encumbrances except as stated herein:

> Covenant against
> Encumbrances

[any exceptions are inserted here]

The Grantor shall not:

[any restrictions imposed by Grantor on Grantee are inserted here]

> Covenant of Seisin

The Grantor is lawfully seized of a good, absolute, and indefeasible estate in fee
simple and has good right, full power, and lawful authority to convey the same
by this deed.

The Grantee, the Grantee's heirs and assigns, shall peaceably and quietly have,
hold, use, occupy, possess, and enjoy the said premises.

> Covenant of
> Quiet Enjoyment

The Grantor shall execute or procure any further necessary assurance of the
title to said premises, and the Grantor will forever warrant and defend the title
to said premises.

> Covenant of Further
> Assurance and Covenant of
> Warranty of Title

In witness whereof, the Grantor has duly executed this deed the day and year
first written above.

_____*Cedric Neal*_____

Use the Right Term

Circle the letter of the choice that best completes each statement. Use the definitions of the terms and your logic to determine the best answer. The answers are shown at the end of the chapter.

1. The legal document that conveys ownership of a property is called a

   _____.

   (a) deed

   (b) covenant

   (c) warranty

   (d) all of the above

2. The most common form of deed is a _____.

   (a) general deed

   (b) grant deed

   (c) warranty deed

   (d) none of the above

3. The type of deed used in California is a _____.

   (a) general deed

   (b) grant deed

   (c) warranty deed

   (d) none of the above

4. A person acquiring ownership of a property is a _____.

   (a) seller

   (b) warranty

   (c) grantee

   (d) grantor

5. "Valuable consideration" could be _____.

   (a) money paid by a buyer of a property

   (b) services rendered

   (c) love and affection

   (d) any of the above

6. A covenant is a _____.

    (a) type of house

    (b) type of deed

    (c) promise or warranty

    (d) grant

7. The covenant that assures a grantee that the grantor owns the property and has the right to sell it is called the Covenant of _____.

    (a) Ownership

    (b) Warranty of Title

    (c) Covenants

    (d) Seisin

8. The type of deed that includes the most warranties protecting the grantee is the _____.

    (a) maximum deed

    (b) grant deed

    (c) warranty deed

    (d) none of the above

9. A deed must include _____.

    (a) consideration

    (b) words of conveyance

    (c) a legal description of the property

    (d) all of the above, and more

10. The Statute of Frauds requires that a deed be _____ .

    (a) valid

    (b) written

    (c) limited to just one property

    (d) all of the above

2. Other Deed Types

bargain and sale deed   guardian deed
correction deed   land patent
gift deed   quitclaim deed

Although warranty deeds and grant deeds are the most common form of deeds, other forms of deeds are used for special purposes.

bargain and sale deed

a deed that contains the minimum essentials of a deed, but no covenants. Grantees acquiring property using such a deed might wish to require title insurance.

correction deed

(also called a *deed of confirmation*) a deed used to correct an error, such as a misspelled name, in an existing deed.

gift deed

a grant deed, warranty deed, or other deed, in which the consideration is "natural love and affection" rather than a sum of money and other valuable consideration.

guardian deed

(also called *guardian's deed*) a deed used to convey a minor's property. A guardian deed contains a covenant that the minor and guardian have not encumbered the property. Such a deed contains a statement that the guardian has the authority to convey the minor's property and names the source of the authority, such as a court order.

land patent

the instrument that conveys a property to an individual from a state or the federal government.

Using Real Estate Terms

Over the course of the nation's history, millions of acres of public land have been granted to miners, settlers, railroads, and colleges by the federal government to foster various activities considered in the public interest. The document used to convey this land was the land patent. ▲▲▲

quitclaim deed

> (also called a *release deed*) a deed by which someone (the grantor) renounces all possession, right, or interest that he or she might have in a property. If the grantor has no right or interest, then none is conveyed. If the grantor does have a right or interest, then that right or interest is conveyed.

Using Real Estate Terms

Michael Benton had owned a house on State Street for more than 15 years before he married Susan. After their marriage, Michael and Susan bought a new house to live in. Michael wanted his old house to be inherited by his sister, and stated so in his will, but his sister was worried that Susan might someday claim the house. Michael asked Susan to sign a quitclaim deed just so that his sister would not worry about any possible future claim by Susan.

▲▲▲

Use the Right Term

Circle the letter of the choice that best completes each statement. Use the definitions of the terms and your logic to determine the best answer. The answers are shown at the end of the chapter.

1. The phrase "natural love and affection" refers to _____.

   (a) the consideration in a gift deed

   (b) the words of conveyance in a gift deed

   (c) the role of the guardian in a guardian deed

   (d) none of the above

2. When property is conveyed from a state to an individual, the form of conveyance is a _____.

   (a) quitclaim deed

   (b) general deed

   (c) gift deed

   (d) land patent

3. A bargain and sale deed _____.

    (a) contains the minimum essential elements of a deed

    (b) contains no covenants

    (c) provides fewer protections for the grantee than a warranty deed

    (d) all of the above

4. A deed with an error such as a misspelled name _____.

    (a) is forever void

    (b) cannot be corrected

    (c) can be corrected with a quitclaim deed

    (d) can be corrected with a correction deed

5. A guardian deed _____.

    (a) contains a statement identifying the guardian's authority to sell the minor's property

    (b) conveys property to the guardian

    (c) names the guardian as grantor and grantee

    (d) is created to protect the guardian

6. Mrs. Whitehead and her brother inherited a property when her parents died. She decides to give her brother her share of the property, and she uses a gift deed to convey it to him. Even though Mrs. Whitehead's husband has no right or interest in the property, she asks him to sign a separate deed releasing all interest that he might have, "just in case." The type of deed that Mr. Whitehead signs is a

    _____.

    (a) gift deed

    (b) grant deed

    (c) estate deed

    (d) quitclaim deed

3. Transferring Land by Will

will

testate

testator/testatrix

holographic will

nuncupative or oral will

codicil

decedant

probate, probate court

executor/executrix

executor's deed

administrator/administratrix

intestate, intestate succession

devise, devisee

bequeath, bequest

legacy, legatee

What happens to a person's interest in a property when he or she dies depends on whether the person had prepared a valid will to indicate how the property was to be distributed. In the absence of a valid will, the person is said to have died intestate, and the property is distributed according to the laws of the state through a court proceeding.

This section presents the terms related to the distribution of property after the death of its owner, whether that person had prepared a valid will or not.

will

> (also called *testament*) a written document specifying how an individual wishes his or her property to be distributed after death. For a will to be recognized as valid, certain legal requirements must be met. In most states, a formal will prepared by an attorney is declared by the will maker to be his or hers and is signed in the presence of two to four witnesses (depending on the state). These precautions help assure that the intentions of the will maker are carried out and reduce the likelihood that the will might be contested or challenged after the person's death.
>
> The maker of a will (*testator* or *testatrix*) may change the will at any time prior to his or her death. Persons named in a will have no right to any property until after the death of the will maker.

testate

> with a will. The common phrase is to say that someone has "died testate" (having prepared a valid will) or "died intestate" (without a will).

testator (male), testatrix (female)

> the maker of a will (testament).

> ## Using Real Estate Terms
>
> Timothy Brown died testate. He had prepared his will several years before he died. In the will, he named his son, Rich Brown, as his executor. The decedent, Timothy Brown, is called the testator because he was the maker of the will. ▲▲▲

holographic will

> a will that is entirely handwritten. A valid holographic will is dated and signed by the will maker. Not all states (only 19 at this writing) recognize holographic wills as legally binding.

> ## Using Real Estate Terms
>
> Norbert Lee prepared his will in his own handwriting, signed and dated it, and gave it to his wife for safe keeping. His will is called a holographic will. ▲▲▲

nuncupative or oral will

> a will made orally when the will maker (testator or testatrix) is near death. Such wills can be valid only for the distribution of personal property, not real property. In such instances, the courts decide the distribution of real property as *intestate succession*.

codicil

> an addendum, supplement, or amendment to a will. The codicil, properly dated, signed, and witnessed, makes changes to a will without the expense or work of rewriting the entire will. This is the only way to change a will without rewriting it.

decedent

> a dead person. This word does not indicate whether the person died with a will (*testate*) or without one (*intestate*).

probate, probate court

> (also called *surrogate court*) the court proceeding whereby the validity of a will is determined and any challenges to the will are presented. The name comes from the Latin term for *prove*, reflecting the procedures whereby a will is proved to be authentic.

executor (male), executrix (female)

> the person named by the will maker (testator) to carry out the instructions in the will.

executor's deed

> a special warranty deed used to convey ownership of a testator's real property. The executor's deed contains a covenant that the executor has not encumbered the property.

administrator (male), administratrix (female)

> a person named by the court to carry out the instructions of a will maker. In some states this person is called a personal representative.

intestate, intestate succession

> without a will. When an individual "dies intestate," that is, dies without a valid will, the courts decide the distribution of the person's property. When this happens, the process is known as *intestate succession* or *title by descent*. The laws of inheritance may vary somewhat from state to state, but usually the surviving spouse and any children of the deceased person receive the property or the largest share of the property, followed by grandchildren, parents, brothers and sisters, and nieces and nephews. These persons are called the heirs or distributes.
>
> If no heirs can be located, the property of the deceased person, the decedent, is taken by the state. (This action is called *escheat*, which is included in Chapter 2.)

Using Real Estate Terms

Otto Ng did without having prepared a will, that is, he died intestate. The courts decided what would happen to Otto's property, based on the laws of the state. ▲▲▲

devise, devisee

> *Devise* is the real property that is willed. The recipient of the real property is called the *devisee*.

Using Real Estate Terms

According to Priscilla Bower's will, her daughter Ann inherited Priscilla's house on Front Street. In this example, Ann is the devisee. The property on Front Street is called the devise. ▲▲▲

bequeath, bequest; legacy, legatee

> to give personal property to an individual by virtue of a will. The personal property so distributed is called a bequest or a legacy. The person receiving the property is called the legatee.

Use the Right Term

Circle the letter of the choice that best completes each statement. Use the definitions of the terms and your logic to determine the best answer. The answers are shown at the end of the chapter.

1. Adam Thornton prepared his "Last Will and Testament" in his own handwriting, signed and dated it, and gave it to his wife for safe keeping. Which of the following is true?

   (a) Adam's wife is the executrix of Adam's will.

   (b) Adam's will is a holographic will.

   (c) Adam's will cannot be a valid will.

   (d) All of the above.

2. Before he died, Adam decided to make some changes to his will. In order for the changes to be valid, Adam could _____.

   (a) mark out the parts he wanted to change, write in the changes, and date and initial the changes

   (b) mark out the parts he wanted to change, and write in the changes

   (c) write an amendment, called a codicil, with the changes, and sign and date the codicil

   (d) tell his wife

3. After Adam's death, the validity of his will was determined by _____.

   (a) his wife and succession court

   (b) his heirs

   (c) his administrator or administratrix

   (d) probate court

4. The job of an executor or executrix is to _____.

   (a) carry out the instructions in the will

   (b) determine the validity of the will

   (c) decide who gets what

   (d) bury the decedent

5. A holographic will _____.

   (a) is made by a person about to die

   (b) is dictated to someone who writes it down

   (c) requires four witnesses to be valid

   (d) is not valid in all states

6. Southy Nelson died without a will. Which of the following is true?

   (a) Southy died intestate.

   (b) Southy prepared a testament.

   (c) Southy had no property to leave to anyone.

   (d) All of the above.

7. On her deathbed, Sarah Brickhouse told her four children to divide everything she owned, giving half to her oldest son and the other half to be divided equally among the remaining three children. One of the children wrote it down almost immediately and submitted it to probate court. Which of the following is true?

   (a) Sarah made an oral will.

   (b) The will was valid only for the dividing of Sarah's personal property.

   (c) The court would make the decisions about her real property according to the state's laws.

   (d) All of the above.

8. The purpose of probate is _____.

   (a) for children to prove they are worthy of inheriting property

   (b) for children to prove they are not minors

   (c) for the court to determine the validity of a will

   (d) to deny anyone the right to challenge any terms of the will

4. Other Ways Land Is Gained or Taken Away

accession	adverse possession
accretion	alienation of title
alluvion, alluvium; reliction	dedication
avulsion	forfeiture of title

accession

change in the extent of an owner's land by natural causes or human actions.

accretion

the gradual accumulation of soil, sand, or rock along the shore of a river, stream, lake, or sea that adds to the extent of the owner's land.

Using Real Estate Terms

To remember the meaning of the word accretion, and to help you distinguish it from other terms describing changes in the extent of land, think of the related term accrual. Accretion is the gradual accrual of sand, rocks, etc. that increase the extent of a property. ▲▲▲

---

alluvion, reliction

two forms of accretion. Alluvion (also called *alluvium* or *alluvial deposit*) is the soil, sand, or mud carried by the water of a stream, river, lake, or sea, and deposited on along a shore. Reliction results from a stream, river, lake, or sea receding from a shoreline and permanently exposing more land.

avulsion

the sudden loss of land along a shore through a violent act of nature. The gradual erosion of a shoreline does not constitute avulsion.

adverse possession

the acquisition of property by having continuous, open, exclusive, hostile possession of it (occupying it) without the owner's permission for an extended period of time in certain circumstances allowed by statute (law). If the claimant has paid property taxes on the property, the claim may be stronger. A claimant to property by adverse possession does not have title to the property that can be conveyed to another unless or until the previous owner has provided a quitclaim deed or a court has quieted the title by decree.

Using Real Estate Terms

For the past six years, Sam Tyler has lived in a house that had been his grandmother's home until her death. Sam's Aunt Catherine holds title to the property, but Sam believes he has right to the property because his grandmother had promised it to him. Now Sam would like to sell the house, but either Catherine must sign a quitclaim deed or a court must quiet the title by decree before Sam can sell it. ▲▲▲

---

alienation of title

> change in ownership.

dedication

> the giving of privately owned land to the public. When a developer divides a parcel into lots and streets, for example, the streets might be given to the town, city, or county. In this way, the local government becomes responsible for the maintenance of the streets. Another example would be the dedication of one parcel of land to a city for its own use (to sell, or to develop a park, school, low-income housing, etc.) in return for the city's approval of development plans on another parcel.

forfeiture of title

> the loss of rights to land when certain conditions of title are not met.

Using Real Estate Terms

Hugo and Mary Ames give land to a university for its use only as agricultural research. They stipulate in the deed that the land must be in continuous agricultural use and that no building may be constructed on it. In the event that the university uses the property to construct a building for any purpose, the rights to the land will be forfeited and will revert to Hugo and Mary or their heirs. ▲▲▲

Use the Right Term

Circle the letter of the choice that best completes each statement. Use the definitions of the terms and your logic to determine the best answer. The answers are shown at the end of the chapter.

1. The stream that runs along the back of William Robins' property has gradually deposited soil and sand on the shore, increasing the extent of the property. Which of the following is true?

    (a) Mr. Robins does not own the additional property. It "belongs to the river."

    (b) Mr. Robins' property has increased by accretion.

    (c) The property has increased by revulsion.

    (d) All of the above

2. Henry and Sarah Martin own a cabin on a lake. Due to environmental changes from global warming, the lake receded. Henry and Sarah built a new boathouse and dock at the "new" edge of the property. Henry and Sarah had the right to build the boathouse and dock

    _____.

    (a) because the land exposed by the lake's receding belongs to them by reliction

    (b) only if they paid the state for the extra land because the state owns the lake

    (c) because the land is alluvion and belongs to them

    (d) only if they dedicated the boathouse and dock to the state

3. Ray Garza and his wife owned a home on an ocean shore cliff. Last summer a hurricane created giant tidal waves that caused the cliffs to collapse, and the Garza home along with them. The term describing this loss of land is _____.

    (a) reliction

    (b) revulsion

    (c) accretion

    (d) avulsion

4. Half of Anthony Beach's barn sits on Anthony Taliaferro's property. This encroachment has been this way for decades, generations in fact,

but nothing was ever said to Mr. Beach about it. Last year Mr. Taliaferro wanted the barn taken down or removed, but Mr. Beach protested and the court let the barn remain. How could this be?

(a) Mr. Taliaferro lost the land by reliction.

(b) Mr. Beach could have been ruled to have ownership of the barn area by reason of adverse possession.

(c) Mr. Taliaferro dedicated the land to the Beach family.

(d) None of the above.

5. Two forms of accretion are _____.

(a) avulsion and revulsion

(b) aversion and recidivism

(c) alluvium and alienation

(d) alluvion and reliction

6. Alienation of title refers to _____.

(a) stealing someone's property

(b) stealing someone's interest in a property

(c) change of ownership

(d) none of the above

Review & Practice: Transfer of Ownership

alluvion	deed
codicil	grantor
correction deed	holographic will
Covenant against Encumbrances	intestate
Covenant of Enjoyment	land patent
decedent	Statute of Frauds

Select the term from the list above that best fits the blank in each sentence below.

1. To make a change to a will, the will maker prepares a _____ and dates and signs it.

2. A _____ is used to correct an error in a deed.

3. According to _____, a deed must be in writing.

4. A person who dies without a will is said to die _____.

5. _____ is the built-up soil deposited on the shoreline by a stream, river, lake, or sea.

6. A handwritten will is a _____.

7. The legal document that conveys ownership of property from one person or entity to another is a _____ .

8. _____ promises that the grantee will have the property free of claims by others.

9. The party that is transferring ownership to another is called the _____.

10. The instrument that conveys a property to an individual from a state or the federal government is _____.

11. _____ promises that the property is clear of encumbrances other than any that might be specifically listed in the deed.

12. _____ refers to a dead person.

Short Answer

Use the space provided to answer the following questions.

1. What is the role of an *executor* or *executrix*?

2. Describe two ways to make a valid change to a will.

3. What is the difference between *alluvion* and *reliction*?

4. Give an example of *dedication*.

5. What is *probate*?

6. What distinguishes a *grant deed* from a *warranty deed*?

7. What is the common consideration specified in a *gift deed*?

8. What is a *grantee*?

9. List five essential elements required for a will to be valid.

10. List the five covenants common to most deeds.

Matching

Match the terms on the left with the statements on the right.

_____ 1. accession

_____ 2. accretion

_____ 3. adverse possession

_____ 4. executor

_____ 5. decedent

_____ 6. codicil

_____ 7. consideration

_____ 8. holographic

_____ 9. intestate

_____ 10. testator

_____ 11. reliction

_____ 12. convey

(a) transfer

(b) handwritten

(c) maker of a will

(d) without a will

(e) changed extent of land by natural causes

(f) gradual accrual of soil

(g) increase of land where a river has receded

(h) addition to a will

(i) value

(j) person named by testator to carry out a will's instructions

(k) dead person

(l) acquisition of property by continuous possession without permission

True or False

Indicate whether each of the following statements is true or false by circling T or F. The answers are shown at the end of the chapter.

T F 1. The most common form of deed is the gift deed.

T F 2. A deed must contain words of conveyance.

T F 3. In a Covenant of Seisin, the grantor promises that he or she owns the property and has the right to sell it.

T F 4. States that use grant deeds include California, Idaho, and North Carolina.

T F 5. The Statute of Frauds requires that wills be in writing and signed.

T F 6. The instrument that conveys a property to an individual from a state or the federal government is a quitclaim deed.

T F 7. A codicil is an addendum, supplement, or amendment to a will.

T F 8. A decedent is a previous claim to a property.

T F 9. Forfeiture of title is the loss of rights to land when certain conditions of title are not met.

T F 10. A correction deed is also called a deed of confirmation.

Answers

Deeds: (1) a; (2) c; (3) b; (4) c; (5) d; (6) c; (7) d; (8) c; (9) d; (10) b

Other Deed Types: (1) a; (2) d; (3) d; (4) d; (5) a; (6) d

Transferring Land by Will: (1) b; (2) c; (3) d; (4) a; (5) d; (6) a; (7) d; (8) c

Other Land Changes: (1) b; (2) a; (3) d; (4) b; (5) d; (6) c

Fill-In
(1) codicil; (2) correction deed; (3) the Statute of Frauds; (4) intestate; (5) alluvion; (6) holographic will; (7) deed; (8) A Covenant of Enjoyment; (9) grantor; (10) a land patent; (11) A Covenant against Encumbrances; (12) decedent

Matching
(1) e; (2) f; (3) l; (4) j; (5) k; (6) h; (7) i; (8) b; (9) d; (10) c; (11) g; (12) a

True or False
(1) F; (2) T; (3) T; (4) F; (5) T; (6) F; (7) T; (8) F; (9) T; (10) T

Chapter 5
PUBLIC RECORDS AND TITLE INSURANCE

How do you know who owns a piece of property? How do you know for certain that Juliet Barnes really owns the gladiolus farm that she is trying to sell you? What would happen if you paid Juliet thousands of dollars, but when you were ready to move to the farm, Benjamin Scott locked the gate and said that he owned the property, not Juliet?

Fortunately, we have public records so that anyone can see who owns a property or who has a recorded claim against a property. When a property is sold or otherwise changes ownership, the new owner should have the ownership put into the public record ("recorded") in the county where the property is located.

The terms covered in this chapter are related to public records, entering information into public records, and searching public records. The chapter also presents terms related to insurance that is issued to protect buyers in the unhappy circumstances of having purchased a property the seller didn't own or have a right to sell.

This chapter is divided into four sections, which address the following: public records and notice of ownership; title; quality of title; and title insurance.

Do You Know These Terms?

abstract of title	lender's policy	record
actual notice	*lis pendens* index	title cloud
chain of title	marketable title	title insurance
color of title	notary public	title report
constructive notice	opinion of title	title search
defect on title	owner's policy	Torrens system
grantor/grantee index	public recorder's office	tract index
inquiry notice	quiet title suit	unrecorded interest

1. Public Records

actual notice	public recorder's office
constructive notice	record
inquiry notice	unrecorded interest
notary public	

A person announces to the world that he or she claims to own a particular property by placing copies of documents in the public record. This is the most common way of giving notice of a claim or right to property. Sometimes a claim is made to a property by occupying or using the property.

Persons who have some claim or rights to a property must make sure that documentation of their rights is filed in the public record. If, for example, Janice Johnson has purchased a home, Janice must make sure that the deed or mortgage or other document showing that rights to the home have been transferred to her is filed in the public record.

While persons who have some claim or rights to a property must record their deed or other document, persons who are interested in obtaining rights to a property have some legal responsibility for finding out about any existing claims to the property. The law recognizes three general forms of knowledge or notice that these interested parties obtain: *constructive* or *legal notice*; *inquiry notice*, and *actual notice*.

actual notice

> notice or knowledge that a person obtains directly by hearing, reading, or observing.

> ## Using Real Estate Terms
> Isabel Downing reads a deed that transfers rights to a property from William Bunting to John Andrews. Now Isabel has actual notice of the deed (and Andrews' claim to the property). ▲▲▲

constructive notice

> the notice that is given to the public by virtue of the availability of public records. The law presumes that because the records are public, all persons are notified. Constructive notice is sometimes called *legal* notice.

inquiry notice

> the notice or knowledge that is acquired by asking specific questions. The law requires a person interested in a property to make reasonable inquiries about any claims or rights to the property.

> ## Using Real Estate Terms
> John Andrews is considering the purchase of William Bunting's farm. He can see a road running across the farm to the river. The law expects John Andrews to inquire about the road, to ask who has rights to use the road, how long it has been there, and other questions concerning it. ▲▲▲

notary public

> a minor officer of the state authorized to administer oaths and to validate identities and signatures on documents that require official witnessing, especially for documents intended to be recorded or filed in the public records. A notary public is one of the persons authorized to take an acknowledgment (formal declaration), which is a requirement prior to recording in nearly all states.

public recorder's office

> the office where documents relating to real estate title are placed or filed for public notice and future reference. The public recorder's office may be called the County Recorder's Office, County Registrar's Office, Bureau of Conveyances, or the Circuit Court Clerk's Office, depending on the terms used in a given county.

The public recorder's office is located in the seat of government of the county. The person in charge at that office may be called the clerk, the registrar, or the recorder.

record

to place a document on file in a designated public office to give public notice of the subject of the document and the parties to the document. Deeds, mortgages, trust deeds, contracts for sale, land contracts, leases, options, liens, easements, and assignments are examples of documents that may be recorded.

Documents brought to the recorder's office to be recorded are photocopied (or perhaps scanned) and returned to their owner. The photocopy or scan is given a number, usually the page number in a book or file, and maintained in chronological order.

To find a recorded document, a person would need to know the page number where it is located or the date on which it was recorded. Since searchers for these documents rarely know this information without assistance, the documents are indexed according to the pertinent parcel of land and according to the name of the grantor or grantee. These indexes are listed in the next section.

unrecorded interest

rights such as month-to-month rentals, leases for a year or less, or easements (see Chapters 2 and 10) or adverse possession (see Chapter 4) claims, which are not recorded.

Use the Right Term

Circle the letter of the choice that best completes each statement. Use the definitions of the terms and your logic to determine the best answer. The answers are shown at the end of the chapter.

1. A deed is recorded _____.

    (a) at the state recorder's office

    (b) at the federal property archives

    (c) at the appropriate county office

    (d) any of the above

2. Three forms of knowledge recognized by law are:
   _____.

   (a) constructive notice, legal notice, and inquiry notice

   (b) legal notice, actual notice, and inquiry notice

   (c) legal notice, actual notice, and written notice

   (d) constructive notice, actual notice, and legal notice

3. Constructive notice is sometimes called _____.

   (a) inquiry notice

   (b) pending notice

   (c) legal notice

   (d) written notice

4. Constructive notice is the notice _____.

   (a) posted on a construction site

   (b) considered given to the public because the public records are available

   (c) given in writing from a seller to a buyer

   (d) none of the above

5. When Joshua Nottingham asked Miles Parker for proof that Miles and his wife Sarah owned the house they had on the market for sale, Miles showed him a deed. The deed transferred the property from the previous owner, Leon Reed, to Miles and Sarah. Joshua read the deed carefully and was satisfied that Miles and Sarah owned the house. Which of the following is true?

   (a) Since Miles had the deed in his possession instead of at the Courthouse, it is not valid. Nottingham should go to the Courthouse.

   (b) Leon Reed is still the owner of the house.

   (c) Joshua Nottingham had actual notice of the Parkers' title.

   (d) All of the above.

6. Inquiry notice is the notice _____.

    (a) temporarily under inquiry by the Court

    (b) the knowledge someone acquires (or should have acquired) by asking questions

    (c) given in writing from a seller to a buyer

    (d) none of the above

7. Although any estate, right, or interest in land can be recorded, some "lesser" rights, such as month-to-month rental interest, are only seldom recorded. These interests are _____.

    (a) invalid interests

    (b) unrecorded interests

    (c) interests under inquiry

    (d) none of the above

8. Joe Rodriguez wants to know the name of the grantee (owner) on the deed of a particular house. He knows approximately when the house was sold. Which of the following approaches will get him the information?

    (a) Take a photo of the house to the county recorder's office and ask the clerk.

    (b) Find the book at the county recorder's office for the year he thinks the house transferred ownership and go through the book page by page.

    (c) Call the local newspaper office and ask them to check their records.

    (d) None of the above.

9. A notary public is _____.

    (a) a minor public official

    (b) authorized to administer oaths

    (c) authorized to validate identities and signatures

    (d) all of these

2. Title

title search	tract index
chain of title	abstract of title
grantee index	opinion of title
grantor index	title report
lis pendens index	

To make sure that a seller actually owns a property and has the right to sell it, someone must search the public records for deeds, liens, easements, and any other information related to the title of the property.

title search

an examination of the public records to assemble the information required to produce a chain of title.

chain of title

the history of the ownership of a property that shows the links of ownership from the current owner back to the original owner. See Figure 5.1 for an example.

grantor/grantee index

a system of indexing recorded documents in alphabetical order according to the grantor (seller or other transferor) or the grantee (buyer or other recipient of the transfer or recording).

In a *grantor index*, all grantors are listed alphabetically for a particular year. Each entry shows, in addition to the grantor's name, the name of the grantee and the location (book and page) where the actual document can be found.

Likewise, in a *grantee index*, all grantees are listed alphabetically for a particular year. Each entry shows, in addition to the grantee's name, the name of the grantor and the location (book and page) where the actual document can be found.

lis pendens index

an index maintained at the office of the County Clerk listing any lawsuits pending against a property. *Lis pendens* is Latin for "pending lawsuits."

Figure 5.1   Chain of Title

Example of Chain of Title

United States Government
To Sarah Powell
By Homestead Act
Recorded 9/14/1880, Bk. XX, pg. Yy

Sarah Powell
To John Littleton and wife Elizabeth
By warranty deed
Recorded 9/28/1910, Bk. XXX, pg. yyy

John Littleton and wife Elizabeth
To Elizabeth Littleton, daughter of John Littleton and wife
Elizabeth
By bargain and sale deed reserving a life estate for the
grantors, John Littleton and wife Elizabeth
Recorded 6/19/1945

John Littleton dies on
8/15/1951
Elizabeth Littleton, wife of John Littleton dies on
8/24/1954

Ann Wilkins, executrix of the estate of Elizabeth Littleton,
daughter of John Littleton and wife Elizabeth
To Sarah Burton
By will
Probated 1/26/1970

Sarah Burton
To John Nottingham Burton
By warranty deed
Recorded 5/22/1986, Bk. XXXX, pg. yyy

tract index

> a system of indexing recorded documents according to the tract of land in which they are located.

> To use a tract index, a person would find the page that lists the recorded mortgages, deeds, or other documents related to the properties in a particular parcel. The user then finds the book and page number where the photocopy or scan of the actual document can be found.

abstract of title

> summary of the recorded documents related to the title to a particular parcel of land. An abstract of title lists the recorded grants, recorded easements, mortgages, tax liens, judgments, etc., related to the title. Each document is summarized and its source (usually book and page number) and date are given.

Using Real Estate Terms

When Ed Saunders was in the process of purchasing a home, the abstract of title on the property listed, among other items, the most current deed, the grantor and grantee named on the deed, the type of deed, a short description of the property, the conditions found in the deed, the date of the deed, and the recording date and book and page number. It also showed information on the grantee's mortgage, including the lender and borrower names and a short description of the mortgage. Because the mortgage had been repaid, the abstract also showed the location (book and page) of the mortgage release document and the date of recording. ▲▲▲

---

opinion of title

> an attorney's opinion, based on review of an abstract of title, as to who is the fee owner of the property. In some states, when this opinion is written and signed by an attorney and attached to the abstract, it is known as a certificate of title.

title report

> a document prepared by a title searcher or abstracter and reviewed by a title company attorney giving the attorney's opinion as to who the fee owner is and listing anyone else identified with a legitimate interest in the property or other right, such as a holder of an easement or a lender. Sometimes the title report is called a *preliminary title report*. This report does not mean the title company is making a commitment to insure the property.

A title report indicates current title, that is, the owner at the time that the title search is conducted. It does not show past ownership. It lists mortgage loans made against the property, but only those loans that have not been (satisfied and) removed from the current records. It also lists other current liens and easements, if any.

Use the Right Term

Circle the letter of the choice that best completes each statement. Use the definitions of the terms and your logic to determine the best answer. The answers are shown at the end of the chapter.

1. Hillary Townsend purchased his home from John Suarez in 1996. Where will the deed be listed (indexed)?

    (a) in the grantee index alphabetically under "Townsend"

    (b) in the tract index for the parcel the home is located in

    (c) in the grantor index alphabetically under "Suarez"

    (d) all of the above

2. Where will the recorded copy of the deed for the above transaction actually be located?

    (a) in the grantee index and the grantor index

    (b) in the public recorder's deed book for 1996

    (c) in the title company office files

    (d) none of the above

3. Chain of title is a _____.

    (a) fence around a newly deeded property

    (b) list of all the transfers of ownership of a property over time

    (c) system of indexing title reports

    (d) deed

4. A title search requires _____.

    (a) a search warrant

    (b) a search of the premises

    (c) a search of the public records

    (d) none of the above

5. Lawyer Daggett reviewed the history of ownership of the old Wessells farm and wrote a report saying that she believed the title to the farm belonged to Henry Wise. Lawyer Daggett's report is called _____.

   (a) a title search

   (b) a title report

   (c) an opinion of title

   (d) an abstract of title

6. A summary of the recorded documents related to the title to a property that lists and summarizes the deeds, easements, tax liens, etc., is called _____.

   (a) a tract index

   (b) a title report

   (c) an abstract of title

   (d) a chain of title

7. The difference between a chain of title and an abstract of title is that _____.

   (a) a chain of title lists the previous ownerships and transfers of ownership and an abstract summarizes all the documents related to those transfers

   (b) an abstract of title lists the previous ownerships and transfers of ownership and a chain of title summarizes all the documents related to those transfers

   (c) a chain of title is tied to an attorney's opinion while an abstract of title is not

   (d) an abstract of title shows only the present ownership while a chain of title summarizes all the documents related to ownership back to the original owner

8. A tract index _____.

   (a) lists all the grantees and grantors of properties in a particular tract

   (b) lists the documents related to all the properties in a particular tract or parcel

    (c) contains copies of all the documents related to all the properties in a particular tract or parcel

    (d) none of the above

9. George Armstrong wants to know if his great-great-grandfather ever owned the house currently owned by Chandler Barnes. The document that would be most helpful to George would be

    _____.

    (a) Chandler Barnes's deed

    (b) a title report

    (c) a chain of title

    (d) none of these

10. Sometimes a title report is called _____ .

    (a) an abstract of title

    (b) a chain of title report

    (c) a preliminary title report

    (d) search of title

3. Quality of Title

marketable title	defect on title
color of title	quiet title suit
cloud on title; title cloud	

Sometimes title to a property is not sufficiently clear for the owner to sell the property and transfer the title. This section deals with the quality of title and various factors that affect it.

marketable title

title that is free from reasonable doubt as to the holder is.

Among the characteristics of a marketable title are that it

- has no undisclosed encumbrances;

- has no serious defects;

- does not expose a buyer to risk of litigation; and

- would be accepted by a reasonable person with assurance of ability to sell or mortgage the property at its market value.

A seller is required to deliver a marketable title at close of escrow.

color of title

title that appears to be good but actually is not.

Using Real Estate Terms

Nancy and Web DiMatteo purchased their home from the Carpenters. Although the DiMatteos did not know it, the Carpenters' deed was a forgery. Nancy and Web held their property under the color of title. ▲▲▲

---

cloud on title; title cloud

a claim, encumbrance, lien, or other impairment on title to a property.

Among the typical examples of clouds on title are

- a recorded contract for deed that a buyer defaulted on but that has not been removed from the record.

- an option that was recorded but not exercised, and that is still on the record.

- a property in which a wife had a dower interest that was sold without a release of that interest from the wife.

- a property whose mortgage was recorded and that was paid in full, but the satisfaction was not recorded.

- a property against which some litigation was pending (see *lis pendens*) but that has been dropped, and has not been removed from the record.

Clouds on title are usually discovered during a title search. Common ways of removing the clouds on title are by quitclaim deed (see Chapter 4) and by *quiet title suit* (see below).

defect on title

(also called *defect of record*) any encumbrance on a title that is recorded, such as a mortgage, an easement, judgments, or deeds of trust; any recorded instrument that would prevent a grantor from giving clear title.

quiet title suit

(or *quiet title action*) legal action to establish title to a property, especially one with a cloud on title. The court decree is recorded, which is notice (legal or constructive notice) of the claimant's interest in the property.

Common reasons for a quiet title suit are for an adverse possessor (see Chapter 4) to establish title and to remove easements and clouds on title. Other reasons are to release a homestead, curtesy or dower interest, and to clear tax titles.

Using Real Estate Terms

Phillip Evans has held adverse possession of a house and ten acres by the bay for the past 15 years. Now he wants to sell the property. To do so, he needs marketable title. So he initiates a quiet title action, asking the court to substantiate his title. ▲▲▲

Use the Right Term

Circle the letter of the choice that best completes each statement. Use the definitions of the terms and your logic to determine the best answer. The answers are shown at the end of the chapter.

1. Edward Faulkner has marketable title to his property. This means that _____.

   (a) he can sell the title but not the land

   (b) he can sell the property and transfer the title without the buyer having to worry about claims against the property

   (c) he needs to initiate a quiet title suit

   (d) none of the above

2. Mike Harmon holds his property under color of title. This means that

   _____.

   (a) Mike is a poacher

   (b) something was wrong with the title that Mike acquired, but he didn't know it at the time

   (c) he must return the property to the person who sold it to him

   (d) none of the above

3. Paula Garcia is purchasing a home from Larry and Ellen Isdell. At one time the Isdells had given Bradford James an option to buy the house, but Bradford never exercised the option and the time period ran out. The option was recorded, however, and it is still part of the public record. Which of the following is true?

(a) The title to the property has a cloud on it.

(b) Only Bradford James can buy the house.

(c) The Isdells own the home under color of title.

(d) None of the above.

4. Art Hurtado and his wife have a mortgage of $92,000 on their home. The mortgage is recorded. This is _____.

(a) a cloud on title

(b) not a cloud because the mortgage is less than $100,000

(c) a defect in title

(d) a quiet title action

5. When the Jankowskis paid off the mortgage on their home, the satisfaction of the mortgage was not recorded. A few years later, they sold their house to the Lintons. The Lintons later discovered that there was a cloud on their title to the property because the ending of the Jankowskis mortgage had not been recorded. Which of the following is the most reasonable course for the Lintons to follow?

(a) Sell their house as quickly as possible before anyone finds out.

(b) Take out a new mortgage.

(c) Buy a marketable title for their property.

(d) Initiate a quiet title suit.

4. Title Insurance

title insurance   owner's policy
lender's policy   Torrens system

Title insurance began primarily as an effort to benefit attorneys if they made errors in interpreting abstracts. Abstracters can make mistakes, and many other things can happen to jeopardize title. A forged deed, the granting of a deed by a minor or incompetent person, a mistaken land description, a missing will later discovered, or confusion from similar names can all result in loss to a property owner. Title insurance is now available to anyone wishing to purchase it.

title insurance

insurance by which a title company warrants against defects in, or liens or encumbrances on, title to real estate. Two types of policies are issued, *owner's policy* and *lender's policy*. (See these terms in this section.)

Title insurance protects against losses from such risks as

- forged deeds, mortgages, or other documents in the chain of title.
- mistaken identification of heirs or unidentified or undisclosed heirs.
- lost or misplaced documents.
- mental incompetence of a grantor.
- lack of majority of a grantor.

lender's policy

a title insurance policy whose proceeds are payable to the mortgage lender and any future holder of the loan. The insurer's liability is limited to the mortgage loan balance as of the date of the claim. Liability is reduced with each mortgage payment and voided when the loan is paid off.

owner's policy

a title insurance policy whose proceeds are payable to the property owner. The coverage in an owner's policy is usually less extensive than in a lender's policy.

Torrens system

a system of land title registration intended to

- simplify the title registration process, and
- provide a title that assures anyone dealing with the property that the only rights or claims that ever need be considered are the ones that are registered.

The Torrens system is allowed in Hawaii, Massachusetts, Minnesota, New York, Colorado, Georgia, North Carolina, Ohio, Virginia, and Washington. The regular title process is *also* allowed in those states. However, once a property is registered with the Torrens system, it must always be registered with that system.

In the Torrens system, the landowner requests a state court to register the property. Notice is given to all interested parties, and, after a search of title is provided to the court, a hearing is held to determine the title status. The court rules in a court decree.

Use the Right Term

Circle the letter of the choice that best completes each statement. Use the definitions of the terms and your logic to determine the best answer. The answers are shown at the end of the chapter.

1. Carl Trower's mortgage is from Martin Mortgage, which holds a title insurance policy on Carl's property. The policy is _____.

   (a) an owner's policy

   (b) a lender's policy

   (c) a lien policy

   (d) a policy of deed

2. Carl also holds a title insurance policy on the property. The policy is _____.

   (a) an owner's policy

   (b) a lender's policy

   (c) a lien policy

   (d) a policy of deed

3. Which of the following does a title insurance policy not cover?

   (a) forged deed in the chain of title

   (b) underaged grantor

   (c) fire, flood, and pestilence

   (d) misfiled mortgage

4. Which of the following is a not true statement?

   (a) The Torrens system is simpler than the "regular" system of title registration.

(b) In the Torrens system, a court decrees the status of a title.

(c) The Torrens system is a title insurance policy.

(d) All of these are true statements.

Review & Practice: Public Records and Title Insurance

abstract of title	marketable title
color of title	notary public
grantor index	owner's policy
inquiry notice	quiet title suit
lender's policy	tract index

Select the term from the list above that best fits the blank in each sentence below.

1. A _____ is a title insurance policy that indemnifies the mortgage holder.

2. Letitia Mears found the deed her great-grandfather signed when he sold the family farm by looking in the _____.

3. To use a _____, a person would find the page that lists the recorded mortgages, deeds, or other documents related to the properties in a particular parcel

4. The coverage in an _____ is usually less extensive than in a lender's policy.

5. A seller is required to deliver a _____ at close of escrow.

6. A legal action to establish title to a property is called _____.

7. Miles and Betty Fisher purchased their home from the Outtens. Although the Fishers did not know it, the Outtens' deed had been signed by a minor. Miles and Betty held their property under the _____.

8. An _____ is a summary of the recorded documents related to the title to a particular parcel of land.

9. The notice or knowledge that is acquired by asking specific questions is _____.

10. A _____ is authorized to administer oaths and to validate identities and signatures on documents that require official witnessing.

Short Answer

Use the space provided to answer the following questions.

1. Why are the grantor, grantee, and tract indexes so important in title searches?

2. Define and give examples of *actual notice* and *inquiry notice*.

3. Define and give examples of *constructive notice*.

4. Define and give an example of *cloud on title*.

5. Describe the *Torrens system* of title registration.

6. What is *lis pendens*? Why is a *lis pendens* index important to a title search?

7. What is meant by *chain of title*?

8. Where is the public recorder's office?

9. What information is contained in a title report?

10. What does title insurance protect against?

True or False

Indicate whether each of the following statements is true or false by circling T or F. The answers are shown at the end of the chapter.

T F 1. Knowledge gained from what a person has seen, heard, read, or observed is called observed knowledge.

T F 2. A person authorized to take acknowledgments is a notary public.

T F 3. A publicly available index that a person can use to learn of pending lawsuits that may affect a title is called a Torrens index.

T F 4. A book at the recorder's office that lists grantors by name is called the alphabetical name index.

T F 5. Chain of title is the linkage of ownership that connects the present owner back to the original source of title.

T F 6. An opinion of title is a complete summary of all recorded documents affecting title to a particular property.

T F 7. Constructive notice is sometimes called legal notice.

T F 8. Actual notice is sometimes called inquiry notice.

T F 9. Cloud on title is the same as color of title.

T F 10. A marketable title is free from reasonable doubt as to who is the owner.

Answers

Public Records: (1) c; (2) b; (3) c; (4) b; (5) c; (6) b; (7) b; (8) b; (9) d

Title: (1) d; (2) b; (3) b; (4) c; (5) c; (6) c; (7) d; (8) b; (9) c; (10) c

Quality of Title: (1) b; (2) b; (3) a; (4) c; (5) d

Title Insurance: (1) b; (2) a; (3) c; (4) d

Fill-In
(1) lender's policy; (2) grantor index; (3) tract index; (4) owner's policy; (5) marketable title; (6) quiet title action; (7) color of title; (8) abstract of title; (9) inquiry notice; (10) notary public

True or False
(1) F; (2) T; (3) F; (4) F; (5) T; (6) F; (7) T; (8) F; (9) F; (10) T

Chapter 6
PURCHASE AGREEMENTS

While the notion of selling a property "on a handshake" may have some romantic appeal, it does little to protect the rights and interests of a buyer or seller. Buyers need to know that a seller actually has the right to sell the property and that the property is in good condition, or at least in the condition represented. They also need time to arrange for the financing of the purchase and to make decisions about inspections and other matters. And, they need to know that once they have made all the payments on the property, they will receive the deed to it. Similarly, sellers need to know that buyers can obtain the financing required within a specified time period. Both buyers and sellers need to specify any other terms or conditions related to the sale of the property. The instrument that provides these protections and specifications is the sales contract—which must be prepared in writing and signed.

The four sections of this chapter address the following: the sales contract, sales contract terms, inspections, and next steps.

Do You Know These Terms?

acceptance	notification
as is	offer to purchase
brokerage commission	perform
buyer default	pest control inspection; termite inspection
close of escrow; closing date	possession
contingency	property description
counteroffer	prorating
damages	purchase agreement
default	purchase contract
deposit receipt	purchase offer
disclosure statement	purchase price
dry rot	riders (addendum, attachment)
earnest money deposit	roof inspection
home inspection	sales contract
instrument	specific performance
latent defects	time is of the essence
liquidated damages	time limits
loan commitment letter	

1. The Sales Contract

instrument	acceptance
sales contract, deposit receipt,	brokerage commission
purchase contract,	earnest money deposit
purchase agreement,	
purchase offer	

The *sales contract* is also called a *deposit receipt*, an *offer and acceptance*, an *offer to purchase*, a *purchase and sales agreement*, a *purchase contract*, and a *purchase offer*. Regardless of what it is called, in most cases the sales contract is prepared using a preprinted form. The form has four main components: an earnest money deposit, an offer to purchase, an acceptance of the offer, and provision for brokerage commission(s).

instrument

a document, usually one intended to make something happen, such as to convey an offer, convey title, make a promise, or restrict an action. Purchase agreements, promissory notes, land contracts, and mortgages are all examples of instruments.

sales contract, deposit receipt, purchase contract, purchase agreement, purchase offer

document that sets forth the terms and conditions of an offer to buy a property and the acceptance of that offer. Also called *offer to purchase*, *offer and acceptance*, and similar phrases.

acceptance

indication by the seller that he or she accepts every detail of the sales contract. Acceptance is shown by the seller's signature at appropriate locations on the sales contract. If the seller rejects any detail of the contract, then the entire contract is considered rejected and the offer is not a binding agreement.

Using Real Estate Terms

Ben Moore receives a sales contract for the purchase of his home by Sukey Brown. Sukey believes that she has made a reasonable offer, but she has included a statement that allows her 90 days to obtain financing. Ben wants the transaction to close in 45 days, so he refuses to sign the contract. In this case, Ben has not accepted the offer and there is no deal. ▲▲▲

---

brokerage commission

amount paid to the broker or brokers providing broker services to the parties. In the past, the seller has customarily paid the commission, however various arrangements are making their way into the real estate transaction process. The amount of the commission and the party responsible for paying the commission is stated in the purchase contract.

earnest money deposit

money submitted by the offeror (buyer) along with a purchase offer. The deposit demonstrates that the buyer is serious about purchasing the property. In most cases, the size of the deposit is not a set amount. Because buyers stand to lose (forfeit) the deposit if they do not meet the terms of the contract, they want to make as small a deposit as possible. The deposit should, however, be large enough that the seller would deem it a significant commitment and risk if the buyer were to forfeit it. Custom varies from region to region, although a deposit of $3,000 to $5,000 on a $120,000 property would seem reasonable in most places. The deposit is at risk only if the seller accepts the offer.

If the buyer meets all terms of the contract, the deposit goes toward the purchase of the property. If the seller defaults on the contract, the deposit is usually returned to the buyer.

Using Real Estate Terms

Sukey Brown included an earnest money deposit of $4,000 along with her purchase offer that was submitted to Ben Moore. But since Ben did not accept Sukey's offer, Sukey did not lose her deposit.

►►►

Frances and Bob Downing included an earnest money deposit of $3,500 along with their offer to buy Theresa Henderson's home. Theresa accepted their offer, but later Frances and Bob changed their minds because they found a different house they liked better. Since they did not complete the transaction, they lost their deposit. ▲▲▲

Use the Right Term

Circle the letter of the choice that best completes each statement. Use the definitions of the terms and your logic to determine the best answer. The answers are shown at the end of the chapter.

1. If a seller accepts everything in a purchase offer except one little detail, _____.

   (a) the contract is a binding agreement

   (b) the offer is considered accepted except for that one detail

   (c) the entire offer is rejected

   (d) the seller must sign the contract

2. If a seller likes everything in a purchase offer, _____.

   (a) the offer is accepted

   (b) the offer is not accepted until the seller signs the contract

   (c) the seller does not need to sign the contract

   (d) none of the above

3. A brokerage commission _____.

   (a) is usually paid by the seller

   (b) is usually paid by the buyer

   (c) is paid half by the buyer and half by the seller

   (d) is illegal

4. An earnest money deposit _____.

   (a) indicates to a seller that the buyer is serious about the offer

   (b) is a small token amount

   (c) is not at risk of being forfeited

   (d) is always completely refundable

5. Which of the following is true?

   (a) A purchase contract is the same thing as a sales contract.

   (b) A purchase contract is the same thing as a purchase agreement.

   (c) A deposit receipt is also called a purchase offer.

   (d) All of the above.

6. Which of the following is true?

   (a) A purchase agreement is an instrument.

   (b) All instruments transfer money.

   (c) All documents are instruments.

   (d) All of the above.

2. Sales Contract Terms

close of escrow; closing date	prorating
contingency	purchase price
loan commitment letter	time is of the essence
property description	time limits

Pre-printed purchase agreements vary from state to state and region to region. Some have grown to be extensive. The terms and conditions included in the various forms vary somewhat, but certain elements are common to most of them.

close of escrow; closing date

> a date, usually specified as a number of days from the acceptance of an offer, by which all required actions are to be completed and title is to be transferred. The actual closing date is the day on which title actually transfers.

contingency

a condition that must be met before a contract is binding. A buyer, for example, may make an offer "contingent on obtaining financing" or "contingent on completed sale of current home."

Using Real Estate Terms

Thomas Scott accepted Elizabeth Upshur's offer to buy his farm. The offer was made "contingent on buyer (Elizabeth Upshur) obtaining financing at a rate of no more than 8.5% within 30 days." Since she did obtain the financing, the contingency was met, and the contract was binding. If Elizabeth had not obtained the financing, the contract would not have been binding. (Elizabeth could receive her deposit back and Thomas could sell the farm to someone else.) ▲▲▲

---

loan commitment letter

a written commitment from a lender to loan the funds to purchase a property.

Using Real Estate Terms

Easy Mortgage Company agreed to finance Elizabeth Upshur's purchase of Thomas Scott's farm. They provided a loan commitment letter to indicate this decision. The actual funds, however, were not sent into escrow until closer to the closing date. ▲▲▲

---

property description

information that clearly identifies the specific property. The property description in a purchase agreement must be one that the state will accept for transferring the title. The key requirement is that the description be clear enough for someone to locate the property and to distinguish the property from any and all other properties. Local custom tends to dictate how this is done. In some areas, for example, the street address plus the assessor's parcel number are used together. Fewer and fewer purchase agreements use the legal description of the property (see Chapter 1).

prorating

the dividing of certain expenses between the seller and the buyer of a property based on the proportion of time of ownership that pertains to that expense. Common expenses that are prorated are property taxes, insurance expenses, utilities, and the like.

Since the seller has paid some of these expenses in advance, the seller is credited for his or her share up until the date of closing.

Likewise, the buyer would be charged for the amount the seller had prepaid.

Some expenses, notably property taxes, are paid *in arrears*, that is, after the fact. The seller still would have to pay his or her share of the property taxes, that is, the tax for the time prior to the date of sale.

The accounting for various prorations happens when the escrow closes. See Chapter 8, Escrow.

purchase price

the amount offered for the purchase of the property. The purchase price does not include fees and expenses related to the transaction; only the price offered for the property. The purchase price *includes* the down payment.

Using Real Estate Terms

Elizabeth Upshur offered Thomas Scott $250,000 for his farm. She plans to make a $50,000 down payment. The purchase price is $250,000 no matter how much down payment she makes. ▲▲▲

Note that the purchase price is the same as the selling price or sale price if Thomas accepts the offer and the property actually sells for that amount.

time is of the essence

a phrase meaning that the time limits written in the contract must be observed or else the contract could be voided. Also, the party that does not meet a time limit may be liable for damages.

Sometimes a buyer or seller will voluntarily grant the other party an extension, but extensions are not required.

time limits

periods of time established to accomplish certain actions. Most purchase offers set a time limit within which the seller must respond. If the seller does not respond by the deadline, the offer is no longer in effect. A short time limit for the seller to respond gives the seller less time to hold out for a better offer.

Other time limits may be stipulated in the purchase agreement as well. Some of these include the time by which a loan must be obtained, the time by which inspections must be completed, and the time by which certain repairs must be made.

Sample Simplified Purchase Agreement

> NOTE: This sample is presented here for illustrative and discussion purposes only. It is not to be used as a form in a real estate transaction.

City of ___Mason___, State of ___(insert State)___. Date: ___May 18, 200X___.
___John Adams___ (Buyer) agrees to purchase and ___Henry Lee___ (Seller) agrees to sell the following real property, located in the City of ___Mason___ , County of___Polk___ , State of _(insert State)_: 1234 Taft Road, a single family residence, legally described as Lot 14, Block A of Monroe Subdivision as per map in Survey Book 8, page 23, in the Office of the County Recorder of Polk County.

The total purchase price is four hundred thousand dollars ($400,000), payable as follows: $12,000 earnest money deposit paid with this Agreement, $68,000 payable by Buyer prior to close of escrow, $320,000 payable by new mortgage on subject property.

Seller will deliver a ___warranty___ deed to subject property to Buyer. Seller will furnish at ___Seller's___ expense a standard title insurance policy to be issued by ___Joe's Title Company___ showing title vested in the Buyer and showing Seller as conveying title free of liens, easements, encumbrances, rights, and conditions, except for ___People's Water Company easement of 26 feet along SE property line___.

The escrow agent shall be___Smith Escrow___. Escrow instructions shall be signed by the Buyer and the Seller and delivered to escrow within five days of receipt. Close of escrow shall be no more than ___30___days after the date of acceptance of this Agreement. Property taxes, property insurance, mortgage interest, income and expense items shall be prorated as of ___close of escrow___.

Any outstanding bonds or assessments shall be paid by the ___Seller___.

Any existing mortgage indebtedness against the property is to be paid by the ___Seller___.

Seller will provide Buyer with a report from a licensed pest inspector that subject property is free of termites and wood rot. The cost of the inspection, report, and any necessary work to be paid by___Seller___.

Possession of subject property to be delivered to the Buyer ___on close of escrow___, at which time all personal property, trash, and debris shall be removed.

Escrow expenses shall be paid by ___Seller and Buyer equally___.

Conveyance tax shall be paid by___Seller___.

Earnest money deposit shall be held ___in escrow___.

All attachments and fixtures now on the premises shall be included.

Other provisions:

If the improvements on subject property are damaged or destroyed prior to close of escrow, or if Buyer is not able to obtain necessary financing, or if Seller is not able to deliver title, then Buyer, at his option, may terminate this agreement and the earnest money deposit shall be returned to him in full. If Seller fails to fulfill any of the other agreements made herein, the Buyer may terminate this agreement with full refund of deposit, may accept lesser performance, or may sue for specific performance.

If this purchase is not completed by reason of Buyer's default, Seller is released from any obligation to sell to Buyer and shall retain the earnest money deposit as his sole right to damages.

Upon the signature of the Buyer, this document becomes an offer to the Seller to purchase the property described herein. Seller has until ___5:00 P.M. May 20, 200X___ to accept this offer as indicated by signing and delivering it to the Buyer. If said acceptance is not received by Buyer by that time, this offer shall be deemed revoked and the deposit shall be returned in full to Buyer.

Time is of the essence in this contract.

Real Estate Broker: ___Rosie's Realty___. By ___Sue Householder___,
7 Beach Road, Mason. (555) 555-5555.

The undersigned offers and agrees to buy the above described property on the terms and conditions herein stated and acknowledges receipt of a copy hereof.

Buyer: John Adams
56 Johnson Way, Mason
(555) 555-1234

ACCEPTANCE

The undersigned accepts the foregoing offer and agrees to sell the property described herein according to the terms and conditions set forth herein.

The undersigned has employed ___Antanna's Realty Services___ as Broker and for Broker's services agrees to pay said Broker as commission the sum of ___twenty-four thousand dollars ($24,000)___, from which amount agent representing Buyer shall be compensated, upon recordation of the deed or if completion of this sale is prevented by Seller. If Buyer prevents completion of this contract, Broker shall share equally in any damages collected by Seller, not to exceed above stated commission.

The undersigned acknowledges receipt of a copy hereof.

Seller: Henry Lee
5055 Central Avenue, Mason
(555) 555-2200
May 18, 200X

NOTIFICATION OF ACCEPTANCE

Receipt of a copy of the foregoing agreement is hereby acknowledged.

Buyer ___John Adams___ Date May 18, 200X

Circle the letter of the choice that best completes each statement. Use the definitions of the terms and your logic to determine the best answer. The answers are shown at the end of the chapter.

1. Valentine Colonna wants to buy Clara and Ray Ayers' house, but she wants to sell her present home first. She makes an offer on the Ayers property that says the offer is good (binding) only if she sells her house in the next 60 days. This condition is called a _____.

   (a) tenancy at sufferance

   (b) contingency

   (c) lease option

   (d) prorating

2. Robert Elliott offers to purchase the home at 8 Seaside Road. Everyone in the area knows that 8 Seaside Road is the old Stith place near the wharf. Which of the following is true?

   (a) Since the location of the property is general knowledge, Robert (or his agent) only has to put "old Stith residence" in the description.

   (b) Robert (or his agent) should indicate that the property is the old Stith residence near the ancient elm tree.

   (c) Even though everyone in the area knows that 8 Seaside Road is the old Stith place, the offer still must include a description of the location of the property that is clear enough that someone from out of the area could locate it.

   (d) Robert must include a metes and bounds description of the property.

3. The sale of the Scott farm is due to close on September 11. Thomas Scott paid the insurance for all of September in advance. Which of the following is true?

   (a) The amount of the insurance will be prorated and Thomas will get a refund of 2/3 (20 days worth) of the fee he paid for September.

   (b) Elizabeth will not be responsible for any insurance until October 1.

   (c) Elizabeth owes Thomas ten days worth of insurance payment based on a proration of the expense.

   (d) Elizabeth must find a new insurance company.

4. Robert Elliot's purchase offer on the old Stith place says "time is of the essence." This means that _____.

   (a) Robert is in a hurry and wants the transaction to be completed in as short a time as possible

   (b) Thomas, who invests in antiques and historic homes, wants a guarantee that the home was built at a certain time

   (c) periodic tenancy

   (d) the time limits specified in the offer agreement must be met or the offer will be void (no good)

3. Inspections

as is

disclosure statement, transfer disclosure
    statement, seller's disclosure statement

pest control inspection, termite inspection

roof inspection

home inspection

dry rot

latent defects

Several clauses in purchase offers are intended to protect buyers against physical problems with a property. Such clauses may specify certain inspections and/or certification(s) to assure, to the extent possible, that the home is free from active pest infestations, roof disrepair, and plumbing, electrical, or other system problems, or, if these problems are present, that the buyer is made aware of them.

as is

in current condition, without any warranty or guarantee or promise to repair. Most homes sold as "real estate owned," that is, being sold by a bank or mortgage company after a foreclosure, and homes sold by reason of a tax lien foreclosure (also called a sheriff's sale), and properties sold in probate, are sold *as is*.

disclosure statement, transfer disclosure statement, seller's disclosure statement

a report completed by a seller and his or her broker indicating the presence and condition of various home features. Some states, California among them, require that this statement be provided to the buyer prior to close of escrow. Furthermore, some states permit sellers to use a home inspection report as a substitute for their own disclosure statement.

Other types of disclosure statements are those provided by a lender to a borrower (which is required by the federal Truth-in-Lending Law), by a broker to a client (agency disclosure), and others.

pest control inspection, termite inspection

examination of a home or other building for the presence of active termites. Many home transactions require such an inspection to be carried out by a licensed pest control inspector, and a clear termite report may be a contingency of the sale. Certain loans, such as FHA, VA, and FmHA loans, require a termite inspection.

Some buyers require a satisfactory termite inspection report or clearance, including repair of certain types of damage and extermination of any live infestations at the seller's expense. Types of termites, infestations, damage, and extermination procedures vary by region.

roof inspection

inspection of the condition of the roof, performed by a roof inspection company, which may or may not also be a roofing company. A termite inspector or home inspector usually will examine the ceiling or roof boards from inside an attic, but not much more.

In some cases, a purchase offer may include a roof inspection clause, asking the seller to certify the condition of the roof and to repair any problems identified by the roof inspection.

home inspection

inspection of a home by a trained professional who examines the major "systems" of the home and reports on their working order. The scope of a home inspection varies from company to company, some of which provide extensive checklists and details.

In most cases, the buyer requests or orders the home inspection and includes a positive or passing home inspection report as a contingency in the purchase offer. Sometimes a seller orders a home inspection and makes the inspection report available to prospective buyers.

dry rot

> wood decay, often from repeated water soakings and/or a fungus. Dry rot is usually identified during a termite inspection, but may also be part of a home inspection. Dry rot turns wood to dust eventually, and may threaten the structural soundness of a building.

latent defects

> defects, usually structural, that are not readily observable during an inspection. Sellers and their brokers are required to disclose latent defects known to them. Failure to disclose known defects can result in voiding of the sales contract and possible legal action.

Using Real Estate Terms

Several weeks after Henry and Tammy Wallace moved into their newly purchased home, they were surprised when the kitchen sink drain clogged. When the plumber came to check the drain, she told the Wallaces that the problem was tree roots growing into the sewer line. She also told them that she had cleared the sewer line about six months earlier for the previous owners, and that she had informed the owners that the roots would grow into the line again soon. This tree root problem is considered a latent defect. In addition, depending on the state in which this occurred, the Wallaces could take some action against the seller, and/or the seller's broker, for failing to disclose the problem. ▲▲▲

Use the Right Term

Circle the letter of the choice that best completes each statement. Use the definitions of the terms and your logic to determine the best answer. The answers are shown at the end of the chapter.

1. *As is* refers to _____.

   (a) a national law stating that it is always the buyer's responsibility to know everything about a house before buying it

   (b) the specific contract phrase "buyer beware," meaning that buyers should be careful

   (c) a clause in all real estate purchase contracts

   (d) a property being sold without any guarantee as to its condition

2. When John Donaldson tore out his old cellar stairs to replace them, he noticed that the beams behind them had developed serious dry rot. Since John is planning to sell his home in the near future, he should _____.

   (a) put back the old steps and say nothing

   (b) put in the new steps and say nothing about the rotting beams

   (c) replace the rotting beams as required by law

   (d) none of the above

3. John decided to put in the new steps, leaving the rotting beams hidden behind the new steps. "If they've been that way this long," says John, "they're not going to hurt anything." When John sells his home, he _____.

   (a) should keep his mouth shut

   (b) should tell the prospective buyers about the rotting beams

   (c) is required by law to repair the beams

   (d) none of the above

4. Ralph Marsh's offer to purchase the Turlington's home included a clause that said the seller must provide a statement showing that the home has no active termite infestation. This clause is _____.

   (a) unreasonable since the Turlington home is mostly brick

   (b) illegal because the Turlington home is more than 50 years old

   (c) common practice and required by law in some states

   (d) none of the above

5. When Andrew Segar made a purchase offer on Hillary Winston's residence, the offer contained a clause requiring a termite inspection. Which of the following is the most likely reason for the clause?

   (a) Andrew could see termite damage around the windows.

   (b) Termite inspections are a common and accepted practice in the course of home sales in that area.

   (c) Andrew wanted to cause trouble for Hillary.

   (d) None of the above.

4. Next Steps

counteroffer   specific performance
rider   default
notification   buyer default
perform   liquidated damages
possession

After a purchase offer has been submitted to a seller, a number of things can happen. The seller might accept the offer, might make a counteroffer, or might decide not to respond at all.

After an offer has been accepted, whether the seller accepts an offer or a buyer accepts a counteroffer, various procedures are set into motion. All parties are notified of the acceptance, escrow is opened (see Chapter 8), a title search is initiated (see Chapter 5), inspections are ordered (see previous section), etc. When all contingencies have been met, the escrow closes and the buyers are given possession of the property according to the terms of the agreement.

If the contingencies specified in a purchase agreement are not met, the escrow may be cancelled. Sometimes problems arise during the course of the escrow, causing the seller or the buyer to default on the contract. This could be something as unpredictable as a change of mind, a job loss, or any number of factors. In this case, escrow is cancelled and appropriate steps are taken, depending on the reason for the default, the terms of the contract, and the decisions of the non-defaulting party.

counteroffer

> an offer made in response to another offer.
>
> The initial counteroffer is made by a seller in response to an offer from a buyer. A counteroffer has the effect of rejecting the original offer and substituting a different offer in its place. By changing even one very small factor in an offer, the entire original offer is rejected.
>
> If a counteroffer is presented to the original offeror, usually the buyer, then the original offeror may accept it (sign it), reject (ignore) it, or prepare a counteroffer to the counteroffer.

Using Real Estate Terms

George Ward did not like the long escrow that was proposed in an offer to purchase his house, although he approved of everything else in the offer. He made a counteroffer to the buyer in which the only change was to shorten the length of the escrow. ▲▲▲

---

rider

> an addendum or attachment to a document, usually initialed by the parties to the document and stapled to it. The document will contain a statement that the rider is a part of it.

notification

> the informing of a buyer that his or her offer has been accepted by the seller (or the informing of a seller that his or her counter offer has been accepted by the buyer). This notification must be in writing and must be acknowledged by the party receiving the notification.

> Some preprinted forms provide a space for the buyer to acknowledge his or her receipt of notification the seller's acceptance.

> Notice that all four steps must be completed before a purchase agreement is a valid contract: offer, acceptance, notification of acceptance, and acknowledgement of acceptance. (In many areas, acknowledgement is effective upon delivery of the notification, and need not be in writing.) In a counteroffer situation, the notification of acceptance and acknowledgement of acceptance follow acceptance by the last party to receive a counteroffer.

perform

> carry out; meet set criteria or requirements. When a party to a contract does not carry out a required action or meet the requirements of the contract, he or she "did not perform."

possession

> physical occupation of a property or control of a property.

> In most property sales transactions, possession of the property passes from the seller to the buyer upon close of escrow or according to specific terms of the purchase agreement.

specific performance

> legal action brought to force a party to carry out the terms of a contract.

default

> failure to perform an action or otherwise complete an obligation specified in a contract.

buyer default

> failure of a buyer, after the signing of a purchase contract, to fulfill his or her obligations as specified in the contract.

liquidated damages

> a dollar amount or a formula for a dollar amount that the parties to a contract agree in advance will constitute the entirety of damages (compensation) to the injured party in the event that one party fails to perform on the contract.

Liquidated damages clauses in real estate purchase contracts limit the amount that can be collected by the seller in the event of a buyer default (see the *buyer default* entry) to a predetermined amount. In some states or areas, that amount is customarily equal to the amount of the earnest money deposit.

Use the Right Term

Circle the letter of the choice that best completes each statement. Use the definitions of the terms and your logic to determine the best answer. The answers are shown at the end of the chapter.

1. Peter and Tabitha Adkins received an offer to purchase their home from Edward Bagwell. Most of the offer was acceptable to them, but they wanted a clause that would allow them to live in the house for six months after the close of escrow, renting it back from Mr. Bagwell. They wrote up a revision of the offer incorporating this additional clause, and it was presented to Mr. Bagwell. Which of the following is known to be true?

    (a) The Adkins prepared and presented a counteroffer to Edward Bagwell.

    (b) Edward Bagwell prepared and presented a counteroffer to Peter and Tabitha Adkins.

    (c) The offer prepared by the Adkins was not legitimate because they are the sellers of the property.

    (d) Mr. Bagwell accepted a counteroffer from the Adkins.

2. Steve Davis made an offer on the Charnock property that was accepted. Before the close of escrow, Steve lost his job. Steve and his wife Polly decided that under the circumstances it would be unwise to purchase the Charnock home. Which of the following statements is known to be true?

    (a) Steve and Polly will probably be sent to jail for failure to perform.

    (b) Steve and Polly might lose their earnest money deposit due to buyer default.

    (c) Steve and Polly did not default on a loan, so there cannot be a penalty.

    (d) Steve and Polly defaulted on their loan and will be required to pay a penalty.

3. Which of the following is a correct order of events?

   (a) offer>counteroffer>notification of acceptance>acknowledgement of notification

   (b) offer>notification of acceptance>counteroffer>acknowledgement of counteroffer

   (c) counteroffer>earnest money deposit>offer>notification of acceptance

   (d) counteroffer>rider>notification of acceptance>acknowledgement of acceptance

4. Which of the following is an example of possession?

   (a) After close of escrow, the Edwards family moves into their new residence on Wednesday, June 30, as stated in the purchase agreement.

   (b) The Fabrizios moved into their new home a week before the close of escrow, as stated in the purchase agreement.

   (c) At close of escrow, Sue Gaetano gave the buyers of her duplex the keys to both units. Both units continued to be occupied by the existing renters.

   (d) All of the above.

5. When Sue Ellen Handy sold her vacation resort property to the Hoffmans, all parties agreed to liquidated damages of $5,000, the amount of the Hoffmans' earnest money deposit. When the Hoffmans defaulted on the contract, which of the following is most likely to have happened?

   (a) The Hoffmans received their earnest money deposit back because the home was a vacation property for Sue Handy, not a primary residence.

   (b) After close of escrow, the Hoffmans took possession of the home.

   (c) Sue Ellen Handy kept the $5,000.

   (d) All of the above.

Review & Practice: Purchase Agreements

as is   loan commitment letter
contingency   notification
earnest money deposit   prorating
latent defects   purchase price
liquidated damages   time is of the essence

Select the term from the list above that best fits the blank in each sentence below.

1. After an offer is accepted, _____ is given to the party that made the offer.

2. Charles Ingram's offer to purchase the old Jarvis place was accompanied by a check for $2,500 to show that he was serious about buying the place. The check was his _____.

3. A clause limiting the dollar amount that a buyer would pay a seller in the event that the buyer defaults on the contract is called a _____ clause.

4. Problems with a house that cannot be seen by a general visual inspection are called _____.

5. A property sold in its current condition, without guarantee or warranty or any promise of repair is said to be sold _____.

6. Evans Justis needed to sell his present house before he could purchase a different one. When he made an offer to buy the family residence of Jonah Krupka, Evans wrote this into his purchase offer as a _____.

7. A phrase used in contracts to indicate that time limits must be met by all parties is _____.

8. Ted Lee's offer to purchase the Mapp residence included a _____ of $230,000, which was a down payment of $50,000 and a loan amount of $180,000.

9. Estelle Merritt's lender sent a _____ to show that her loan had been approved.

10. When their escrow closed on February 18, a seller and buyer agreed that the seller would pay 18/28ths of the month's water bill and the buyer would pay 10/28ths of it. This division of the expense is called _____.

Use the space provided to answer the following questions.

1. What is the difference between a *home inspection* and a *termite inspection*?

2. Define and give an example of *buyer default*.

3. What is *dry rot?*

4. Give an example of a *latent defect*.

5. Under what conditions does a *specific performance* occur?

6. What is a *brokerage commission*?

7. List four names for a *purchase agreement*.

8. What is a *rider*?

9. Explain the difference between *notification* and *acknowledgement of notification*.

10. What is the purpose of a *disclosure statement*?

True or False

Indicate whether each of the following statements is true or false by circling T or F. The answers are shown at the end of the chapter.

T F 1. If one small term of a purchase offer is rejected, the offer is not considered accepted.

T F 2. A deposit receipt is a completed, accepted agreement of purchase.

T F 3. Federal law requires every property to be inspected for live infestations of pests prior to sale.

T F 4. A deposit receipt is an instrument.

T F 5. A seller is required to give possession of a property to the buyer upon acceptance of the purchase offer.

T F 6. Liquidated damages and latent defects are equivalent terms.

T F 7. A loan commitment letter does not necessarily mean that the loan funds have been sent into escrow.

T F 8. The property description on a purchase offer must include the full metes and bounds legal description.

T F 9. A sales contract is different from a purchase contract.

T F 10. When a seller does not like all of the terms of a purchase offer, he or she may accept just the ones that are acceptable.

Answers

The Sales Contract: (1) c; (2) c; (3) a; (4) a; (5) d; (6) a

Sales Contract Terms: (1) b; (2) c; (3) a; (4) d

Inspections: (1) d; (2) d; (3) b; (4) c; (5) b

Next Steps: (1) a; (2) b; (3) a; (4) d; (5) c

Fill-In
(1) notification; (2) earnest money; (3) liquidated damages;
(4) latent defects; (5) as is; (6) contingency; (7) time is of the essence;
(8) purchase price; (9) loan commitment letter; (10) prorating

True or False
(1) T; (2) F; (3) F; (4) T; (5) F; (6) F; (7) T; (8) F; (9) F; (10) F

Chapter 7
EXCHANGES AND OTHER AGREEMENTS

Although a purchase agreement may be the most common way that property changes owners, various other means are used to accomplish similar results. Exchanges of property, lease-option agreements, and installment contracts are not uncommon. Furthermore, letters of intent and binders perform important functions in many real estate transactions.

This chapter is divided into four sections, addressing the following: installment contracts, lease-options, exchanges, and related instruments.

Do You Know These Terms?

bill of sale

binder

conditional sales contract

contract for deed

delayed exchange

equitable title

exercise an option

installment contract

land contract

lease-option

letter of intent

option fee

optionee

optionor

qualified intermediary

right of first refusal

tax-deferred exchange

trading up

vendee

vendor

1. Installment Contracts

conditional sales contract

contract for deed

installment contract

land contract

equitable title

vendee

vendor

conditional sales contract

also called *contract for deed*, *installment contract*, or *land contract*. an agreement between a buyer and a seller of real property wherein part or all of the payment is deferred. The deed to the property is not delivered to the buyer until all payment has been made. The buyer does, however, have possession of the property and holds equitable title (see below) during the time between the date of the agreement and the final payment.

Payments are made to the seller of the property. This arrangement is advantageous for buyers who may have difficulty qualifying for a mortgage. It also holds certain tax advantages for sellers since they can defer payment of a portion of tax.

This type of agreement was most commonly used for selling bare land and was usually called a land contract. As it came to be used more frequently for properties with homes, however, the other names came into use.

In this type of contract, the seller is called a *vendor* and the buyer is called the *vendee*.

equitable title

the title held by a vendee in an installment contract until such time as all payments have been made and the vendor delivers good legal title via the deed. During the time period in which the vendee holds equitable title, the vendor holds "bare" or "naked" title, that is, title in name only and without full ownership rights, most notably, possession..

vendee

> a buyer. In real estate, this term for a buyer is used most commonly with reference to the buyer in an installment contract.

vendor

> a seller. In real estate, this term for a seller is used most commonly with reference to the seller in an installment contract.

Using Real Estate Terms

Irwin and Tammy Parks agreed to sell their home near the Nassawadox Creek to newlyweds Bud and Janet Long. The young couple's credit history was insufficient to qualify them for a home loan from the bank, so the Parks agreed to an installment sale. Bud and Janet Long, the vendees, will occupy the house while they make payments to the Parks, the vendors. During this time, Bud and Janet Long hold equitable title, and Irwin and Tammy Parks hold bare legal title. When the final payment is made, the Parks will deliver the deed to the Longs. ▲▲▲

Use the Right Term

Circle the letter of the choice that best completes each statement. Use the definitions of the terms and your logic to determine the best answer. The answers are shown at the end of the chapter.

1. An advantage of buying a property by an installment sale is that the

    _____.

    (a) vendor occupies the property

    (b) vendor gets all of his or her money at once

    (c) vendee gets clear title at the time the contract is signed

    (d) vendee can purchase the property even if his credit isn't sufficient for a bank loan

2. Under an installment contract, the _____ until the final payment has been made.

    (a) vendor retains bare legal title

(b) vendee has bare legal title

(c) vendor retains equitable title

(d) none of these

3. Julia Ann Rogers is selling her property in Craddockville to Bob Turner by means of a land contract. Which of the following is known to be true?

    (a) Julia Ann is the vendee.

    (b) Julia Ann owns the property as a life estate.

    (c) There is no house on Julia Ann's property.

    (d) Bob will make payments to Julia Ann.

4. Using the same example, which of the following is true?

    (a) This is an installment sale.

    (b) Bob Turner holds bare legal title.

    (c) Julia Ann Rogers holds equitable title.

    (d) None of the above.

2. Lease-Options

lease-option	optionor
exercise an option	option fee
optionee	right of first refusal

lease-option

also called a *lease with option to buy*. an agreement between the owner of a property (lessor) and a tenant (lessee) that allows the tenant to buy the property at a particular price within a certain period of time, usually a year.

In other words, the lease-option gives the tenant a right to purchase the property at a specific price up until a certain date. The tenant is not required to purchase the property, but the owner is required to sell it if the tenant decides to buy it according to the terms of the lease-option agreement. Furthermore, the owner cannot sell the property to anyone else during the period that the lease-option is in effect.

If and when the tenant decides to purchase the property under the lease-option agreement, the tenant gives the owner notice of intent to exercise the option to buy.

In some cases, the rent or a portion of the rent that the tenant pays the owner goes toward the purchase price of the property. This is not true in all cases, however, and this point must be covered in the lease-option agreement.

exercise an option

to take advantage of an opportunity; to activate a choice. In real estate, the phrase usually refers to a lease with option to buy, or lease-option.

optionee

the person or entity receiving the option. In a lease-option, this is the tenant (lessee).

optionor

the person or entity giving the option. In a lease-option, this is the owner (lessor).

Using Real Estate Terms

When Bill Sturgis leased his house on Plantation Creek to the Bibbins, they all signed a lease-option agreement. This gave the Bibbinses (called the optionees) a right to purchase the house from Bill Sturgis (the optionor) for $234,000 any time during the first year of the lease.

About four months later, the Bibbinses decided to exercise their option to purchase the property. They sent the optionor, Bill Sturgis, a notice of their intent to exercise the option, and Bill sold them the house.

A few weeks earlier, Murphy Kellogg had offered Bill Sturgis $250,000 for the property, but Bill could not sell the house to Murphy because he had given the Bibbinses the option. ▴▴▴

---

option fee

an amount of money that an owner can charge the tenant for the privilege of having the exclusive right to purchase the property according to the terms of the lease-option agreement.

right of first refusal

the right to be given an opportunity to purchase a property before anyone else does.

Tenants who have been given a right of first refusal are somewhat protected from having their premises sold to someone else without their knowledge. This is especially important to persons or businesses who would want to purchase given the opportunity.

In practice, this usually takes the form of an owner receiving an offer from another party and showing that offer to the tenant who has the right of first refusal, giving him or her the opportunity to match the offer. If the tenant decides against matching the offer, then the owner is free to accept the offer in hand (and the right of first refusal is no longer in effect).

Use the Right Term

Circle the letter of the choice that best completes each statement. Use the definitions of the terms and your logic to determine the best answer. The answers are shown at the end of the chapter.

1. Mark Valdez leases a home to Mary Elizabeth and William Wharton. He and the Whartons signed a lease-option agreement. Which of the following statements is true?

   (a) The Whartons have a right to purchase the house from Mark Valdez for a certain price up until a certain date.

   (b) If the Whartons decide to purchase the house, Mark Valdez will set the price at that time.

   (c) Mark Valdez can sell his house whenever he wishes and to whomever he wishes.

   (d) The Whartons cannot afford to buy the house.

2. The Whartons decide to buy Mark Valdez's house. They are exercising

   _____.

   (a) their option

   (b) their right of first refusal

   (c) their rights as optionors

   (d) bad judgment

3. Anne Young would agree to lease the corner store in Marionville for her antique shop only if the owner would sign a right of first refusal agreement. Why would Anne insist on this?

(a) She does not want to deal with the potential changes and problems of new ownership.

(b) She would want the opportunity to purchase the property if the owner would consider selling it.

(c) Either of these reasons.

(d) Neither of these reasons.

4. George Addison has a lease-option agreement with his landlord, Chris Beckett, owner of the house George occupies. Chris agreed to give George the lease-option agreement, but he required George to pay him an extra $50 per month on his rent in return. This extra $50 is _____.

(a) extortion

(b) an option fee

(c) a bonus

(d) a lease fee

5. In the above example, Chris Beckett is _____.

(a) lessor, landlord, optionor, owner, and possible seller

(b) lessor, landlord, optionee, owner, and possible seller

(c) lessee, tenant, optionor, and possible seller

(d) lessor, tenant, optionee, owner, and possible seller

6. In the above example, George Addison is _____.

(a) lessor, tenant, optionee, and possible buyer

(b) lessee, tenant, optionor, and possible buyer

(c) lessee, tenant, optionee, and possible buyer

(d) none of the above

7. Floyd Chandler leases his home from Clara Drummond. Floyd has an agreement with Clara that says if she receives an offer to purchase the house, she would give Floyd an opportunity to match the offer and buy the house himself. This arrangement is called

   _____.

   (a) collusion

   (b) lease with option to buy

   (c) right of first refusal

   (d) price fixing

8. In the above example, Tom Ewell offers Clara $190,000 for the house. Clara shows Floyd the offer from Tom, and Floyd says he'll match it. What happens next?

   (a) Clara sells the house to Tom because he offered first.

   (b) Clara sells the house to Floyd because Floyd holds right of first refusal.

   (c) Clara sells the house to Floyd because Floyd holds a lease-option agreement.

   (d) Clara decides to sell the house to Gina Fisher.

3. Exchanges

delayed exchange   tax-deferred exchange
qualified intermediary   trading up

Trading property for property, instead of property for money, has several appealing characteristics. Some exchanges can result in trading a currently owned property for a desired property without using a lot of cash. Also, an owner can dispose of a current property and acquire a different one while deferring income taxes on the capital gain from the first property. This section treats some of the important terms related to exchanging property.

delayed exchange

a nonsimultaneous exchange; exchange of a property in return for a right to acquire a property at some time in the future. The IRS will allow a nonsimultaneous exchange to be tax-deferred if it meets three requirements:

(a) the designated property must be identified within 45 days of the closing of the original property;

(b) the title to the designated property must be acquired (transferred) within 180 days of the closing of the original property;

(c) the designated property is received before the designating party's tax return is due.

Using Real Estate Terms

Wayne Gladden is willing to exchange his small office building for another property, but he hasn't yet found the property he'd like to acquire. Reuben and Mary Westerhouse would like to acquire Wayne's building. A delayed exchange gives Wayne the right to find a suitable property and designate it and take title to it after the closing, if he meets the three requirements.

1. The Westerhouses acquired Wayne's building on May 15, and Wayne identified a building he would like to acquire on June 25. This was within the 45-day limit.

2. Wayne gained title to the designated property on August 20. This was within the allowed 180-day period after the closing of the original property on May 15.

3. Wayne gained title to the designated property more than ten days before his tax return was due (April 15 of the following year). ▲▲▲

---

qualified intermediary

a person or entity holding and controlling the funds and closing documents related to an exchange, in accordance with an escrow agreement between the parties exchanging properties.

tax-deferred exchange

the exchange of one property for another to result in a nontaxable gain. The two properties must be investment properties. (The IRS has other provisions for homeowners to sell their residences and exclude gains within certain limits.)

In a tax-deferred exchange, no taxes are due at the time of the exchange. Taxes will be due, however, when the acquired property is eventually sold for cash rather than exchanged.

Using Real Estate Terms

Sally Evans owns a duplex in Parkford, and she wishes to exchange it for a triplex in Southville. The value of the duplex on Sally's accounting books is $130,000, but its market value is $180,000. If Sally sells the duplex for cash, she will have to pay income tax on the difference between the amount on her books ($130,000) and the amount she receives for it (say $180,000), that is, $50,000.

Sally finds a triplex in Southville valued at $180,000. If Sally exchanges her duplex with a value on her accounting books of $130,000 for the triplex in Southville, the triplex acquires the accounting book value of Sally's original property (the duplex) or $130,000. In effect, Sally did not gain $50,000 in this arrangement, so she owes no income tax on the exchange.

Some time later, Sally decides to sell the triplex for cash. She will owe tax on the gain, that is, the amount over $130,000 that she gets for the triplex. ▲▲▲

---

trading up

> an exchange involving properties that are not of equal value.

Using Real Estate Terms

The small bed and breakfast owned by William Langford has a market value of $200,000. William owns it free of debt. He may exchange it for another property worth, for example, $500,000 that has $300,000 of debt against it. If he does this, William will be trading up. ▲▲▲

Use the Right Term

Circle the letter of the choice that best completes each statement. Use the definitions of the terms and your logic to determine the best answer. The answers are shown at the end of the chapter.

1. An exchange of property in which the owner exchanges a current property now in return for another property in the near future is called _____.

   (a) a delayed exchange

   (b) a dominant exchange

   (c) exchange divisible

   (d) tax evasion

2. A qualified intermediary _____.

    (a) is a property that qualifies for an exchange

    (b) is an arbitration manager

    (c) must follow the instructions of the escrow agreement

    (d) none of the above

3. The exchange of one property for another to result in a nontaxable gain is called _____.

    (a) trading up

    (b) illegal by the IRS

    (c) a tax-deferred exchange

    (d) an intermediate sale

4. In a tax-deferred exchange, _____.

    (a) no taxes are due at the time of the exchange

    (b) the acquired property assumes the value of the original property

    (c) taxes will be due when the acquired property is eventually sold for cash

    (d) all of the above

4. Related Instruments

bill of sale   letter of intent
binder

bill of sale

a document showing the transfer of personal property. A bill of sale usually contains a description of the item(s), the amount being paid (consideration), the name of the selling and buying parties, the date, and the signature of the seller.

Occasionally, an item of personal property, such as a washer and dryer or refrigerator or yard art, will be listed on a real estate purchase contract, even though technically it should be transferred on a bill of sale.

binder

> a short contract used in some areas of the country to hold a real estate transaction together until a more detailed purchase contract can be drawn up and signed.
>
> A binder is a legally binding contract. It usually does not, however, contain the important details found in a purchase contract, such as provisions regarding inspections, the type of deed that the seller will deliver, closing date, and certain other terms and conditions.

letter of intent

> a document that describes the intent of two or more parties to buy, sell, lease, or otherwise agree on a transaction related to a property but without creating a legally binding obligation. A letter of intent is not a contract, but it usually indicates that the parties will go forward with the transaction in good faith.
>
> Letters of intent are most commonly used in commercial leases, construction projects, real estate development, and with sales of very high dollar (millions of dollars) properties.

Use the Right Term

Circle the letter of the choice that best completes each statement. Use the definitions of the terms and your logic to determine the best answer. The answers are shown at the end of the chapter.

1. John Hyslop would like to include the purchase of some workshop power tools when he buys Joe and Sofia Hernandez's home. Which of the following is true?

   (a) John cannot buy the tools.

   (b) John can buy the tools on a bill of sale.

   (c) The tools will automatically be included on the purchase contract for the house.

   (d) None of the above.

2. Minnie Joynes and Harold Kellam have signed a binder for the sale of Minnie's home by Ki's pond to Harold. Which of the following is true?

    (a) They still need to agree to additional terms and conditions and sign a purchase contract.

    (b) Either party can back out of the deal at any time because the binder is not a legally binding contract.

    (c) The binder is not valid because the property is on a waterfront.

    (d) None of the above.

3. A letter of intent is _____.

    (a) a binder

    (b) a bill of sale

    (c) a land patent

    (d) none of the above

4. Which of the following is a true statement?

    (a) A bill of sale cannot be used to sell a refrigerator.

    (b) A contract for sale of real property can include sale of a refrigerator.

    (c) A refrigerator is real property.

    (d) None of these.

Review & Practice: Exchanges and Other Agreements

bill of sale	lease-option
binder	naked title to property
equitable title	optionor
exercise an option	right of first refusal
installment contract	trading up

Select the term from the list above that best fits the blank in each sentence below.

Ted Matthews is purchasing a home from Ted Moore. The two Teds have an agreement that Matthews will make payments to Moore, and when all payments have been made, Moore will deliver the deed. Meanwhile, Matthews will live in the home. Answer the questions below based on this information.

1. Until the final payment is made, Ted Matthews holds
   _____ to the property.

2. Until the final payment is made, Ted Moore holds
   _____.

3. The agreement between the two Teds is called
   _____.

Sonja Rew has an agreement with her tenants, Stu and Sue Paulo, that if they want to buy the house they occupy within the first year of their living in it, they may do so at a purchase price of $280,000. Based on this information, complete the following.

4. The agreement between Miss Rew and Mr. and Mrs. Paulo is
   _____.

5. The Paulos have a year within which to _____.

6. Relative to this agreement, Miss Rew is the _____.

Complete each of the following:

7. Miss Rew rents another house to the Shaws. She has agreed that if she decides to sell the house and she gets an offer, she will give the Shaws the opportunity to match the offer. This agreement is called
   _____.

8. Bill Taylor wants to exchange his small medical building for a larger one across town. To do this, he will have to assume some debt or add some cash into the exchange because the larger building has higher market value. This transaction is called _____.

9. An instrument commonly used for the transfer of personal property is a
   _____.

10. A short contract used until a more detailed purchase contract can be executed is a _____.

Use the space provided to answer the following questions.

1. What is the difference between a *purchase contract* and a *binder*?

2. Define and give an example of *right of first refusal*.

3. Define and give an example of a *tax-deferred exchange*.

4. What is meant by *exercising an option* to buy?

5. Under what conditions does an individual hold *equitable title*?

6. Explain the difference between a *lease-option* and a *right of first refusal*.

7. List three other names for an *installment contract*.

8. What is the role of a *qualified intermediary* in an exchange?

9. Explain the difference between a *optionee* and a *optionor*.

10. Explain the difference between a *binder* and a *letter of intent*.

True or False

Indicate whether each of the following statements is true or false by circling T or F. The answers are shown at the end of the chapter.

T F 1. The advantage of buying a property by an installment sale is that the vendor gets all the money up front.

T F 2. A land contract is used exclusively for the sale of bare land.

T F 3. An installment contract is a means for a seller to defer payment of capital gains tax.

T F 4. A tax-deferred exchange contract is a means for a seller to defer payment of capital gains tax.

T F 5. Tenants hold equitable title to the premises they are renting.

T F 6. Under the terms of a contract for deed, the deed to the property is not delivered to the buyer until the final payment has been made.

T F 7. In a delayed exchange, the buyer is called the vendee and the seller is called the vendor.

T F 8. Tax-deferred exchanges are intended for investment property transactions only.

T F 9. In a delayed exchange, the owner of a property disposes of his or her property at one point in time and can acquire the other property later.

T F 10. Properties involved in a delayed exchange and in trading up are not of equal value.

Answers

Installment Contracts: (1) d; (2) b; (3) d; (4) a

Lease-Options: (1) a; (2) a; (3) c; (4) b; (5) a; (6) c; (7) c; (8) b

Exchanges: (1) a; (2) c; (3) c; (4) d

Related Instruments: (1) c; (2) a; (3) d; (4) b

Fill-In
(1) equitable title; (2) naked title to the property; (3) an installment contract; (4) a lease-option; (5) exercise an option; (6) optionor; (7) right of first refusal; (8) trading up; (9) bill of sale; (10) binder

True or False
(1) F; (2) F; (3) T; (4) T; (5) F; (6) T; (7) F; (8) T; (9) T; (10) F

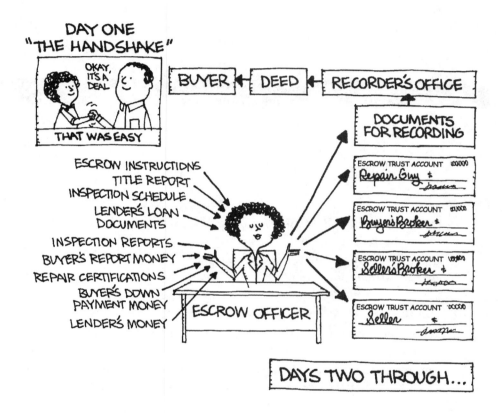

From the time that a buyer and a seller agree to the terms of a real estate transaction, usually indicated by signing a purchase agreement (sales contract), to the time that the title of the property is actually transferred to the buyer, many steps happen. Inspections of the property and repairs are made. The title search is carried out (see Chapter 5). The buyers arrange for a loan. Tax and other amounts are estimated and divided appropriately between buyer and seller. Escrow ensures that all the steps are carried out by a neutral third party.

Do You Know These Terms?

beneficiary statement	escrow fees
close into escrow (dry closing)	escrow instructions
closing costs	escrow officer
closing date	good faith estimate
closing meeting	outside of escrow
closing statement	prorating
concurrent recording	RESPA
escrow	settlement statement
escrow agent	walk-through
escrow closing	

1. Escrow: Basic Terms

escrow	escrow closing
escrow agent (officer)	escrow fees
escrow instructions	outside of escrow

escrow

the process of collecting and distributing the funds and documents needed to complete a real estate transaction. Escrow services are performed by a neutral third party called the *escrow agent* or *escrow officer.*

escrow agent or escrow officer

an employee of an escrow company with the primary responsibility of ensuring that the parties have delivered all documents and money necessary to complete a transaction and that they have complied with all other terms of the escrow instructions.

The duties of the escrow agent begin with placement of the buyer's earnest money deposit in a trust account and preparation of the *escrow instructions* for the buyer and seller to sign. The escrow instructions list in writing everything that the buyer and the seller must do before the deed can be given to the buyer.

When all terms of the escrow are met, the escrow officer authorizes the recording of the documents to transfer title to the property to the buyer(s).

escrow instructions

a document executed by all parties to a transaction in which the escrow company is authorized to collect money and documents from the parties and perform other acts as agreed by the parties.

In residential sales transactions, escrow instructions are usually derived from the terms of the purchase contract.

Escrow instructions include the following information:

1. A list of the documents, funds, and other items to be placed into escrow. The list indicates who is placing each item into the escrow.
2. A list of the conditions that must be met by the buyer and the seller prior to escrow's closing. Conditions might include financing, inspections, repairs, and other requirements.
3. A list of fees and other expenses that will be shared (prorated) by the buyer and the seller. Such expenses might include insurance, rents, and property taxes.
4. A clear explanation of all amounts to be paid by the principals of the transaction to the escrow.

escrow closing

the final transfer of ownership of real property from one party to another. In some locations, closings occur in an attorney's office; elsewhere, closings transpire in an escrow office, broker's office, or recorder's office.

The escrow agent orders the recording of the transfer of title, along with the deed, mortgage, and any other documents to be recorded as part of the transaction. When the recording is confirmed, the escrow agent gives or sends a check to all the parties to whom funds are due, such as the seller, the real estate brokers, etc. The recorded deed is usually sent to the buyer and the mortgage release to the seller and the new mortgage to the lender several days later.

escrow fees

the charges imposed on the parties to an escrow by the escrow company for the processing of a transaction. In many residential sales transactions, escrow fees are split equally between the buyer and the seller.

outside of escrow

agreements, payments, or acts connected with a real estate transaction that are performed separately from the escrow instructions and about which the escrow is not concerned.

Using Real Estate Terms

When she purchased Thomas Moreland's house, Sandra Ballinger also purchased several oil paintings from Thomas that were hung in the dining area. She negotiated the purchase of the paintings herself and paid Thomas directly. No mention of the paintings was made in the purchase offer on the home nor in the escrow instructions. Sandra handled the purchase outside of escrow. ▲▲▲

Use the Right Term

Circle the letter of the choice that best completes each statement. Use the definitions of the terms and your logic to determine the best answer. The answers are shown at the end of the chapter.

1. Escrow services are performed by _____.

   (a) the buyer's real estate agent because it's the buyer's money

   (b) the seller's agent because it's the seller's property

   (c) neither the buyer's agent nor the seller's agent because they are not neutral

   (d) none of the above

2. An escrow agent or escrow officer _____.

   (a) authorizes the recording of the documents to transfer title

   (b) ensures that the parties have delivered all documents and money necessary to complete a transaction

   (c) ensures that the parties have complied with all other terms of the escrow instructions

   (d) all of these

3. Which of the following items is/are included in escrow instructions?

   (a) a list of the conditions that must be met by the buyer and seller prior to completion of the transaction

   (b) analysis of the credit data collected by the lender

   (c) the escrow agent's rate of pay

   (d) none of these

4. Ted Freidman sold his house and his boat to Jack Winters. The sale of the boat was not included in the purchase agreement with the sale of the house. Which of the following is true?

   (a) Ted sold the boat outside of escrow.

   (b) Ted sold the boat inside of escrow.

   (c) Jack bought the boat illegally.

   (d) None of these.

2. Escrow: Money

closing costs
good faith estimate of closing costs
prorating

RESPA
closing (or "settlement") statement

closing costs

expenses of consummating a real estate transaction that are separate from the actual price of the property. Closing costs, which may be owed by both buyer and seller, vary in different locations, but may include loan fees and points, escrow and title costs, termite and radon inspections and corrective measures, attorney's fees, home warranties, association transfer fees, appraisal charges, and brokers' commissions.

good faith estimate of closing costs

an estimate of closing costs given to a borrower by a lender so the borrower can compare prices of the services to be used for the transaction. See Figure 8.1. Note that some costs and/or items vary by local custom.

prorating

assigning a portion of a cost or a benefit to two or more parties. Escrow officers must generally prorate taxes, association dues, interest, and insurance between the buyer and seller at the close of escrow. Prorating ensures that each party pays his or her fair share of the costs.

Using Real Estate Terms

Betty Mason pays her taxes in advance for a full year. When she sold her house to Charlotte Neville mid-year, the escrow officer gave Betty a credit from the buyer of an amount equal to half the year's taxes. ▲▲▲

▶▶▶

Daniel Martin sold his duplex to Evan Parker. The escrow closed on the 10th of September. The escrow officer prorated the rents so that Daniel received one third and Evan received two thirds. Likewise, the gardener expenses and trash and sewer costs were prorated so that both the buyer and the seller paid their share. ▲▲▲

Figure 8.1 Sample Closing Costs Estimate Form

ABC LENDING COMPANY Good Faith Estimate of Closing Costs Prepared for Mr. and Mrs. Buyer	
TYPE OF COST	ESTIMATED COST
Loan origination fee	$
Loan discount	
Appraisal fee	
Credit report	
Lender's inspection fee	
Interest	
Mortgage insurance application fee	
Loan assumption fee	
Tax service fee	
Interest	
Mortgage insurance premium	
Notary fees	
Title insurance, lender's coverage	
Title insurance, owner's coverage	
Recording fees	
County tax	
City tax	
Pest inspection fee	
Building/home inspection fee	
TOTAL	$

RESPA

> abbreviation for Real Estate Settlement Procedures Act, which applies to transactions involving federally related first mortgage loans such as FHA or VA or other government-backed or assisted loans and certain other loans.
>
> This 1975 federal law (revised significantly in 1997) requires the disclosure to borrowers on residential one- to four-unit properties of settlement (closing) procedures and loan costs by means of a pamphlet and forms prescribed by the U.S. Department of Housing and Urban Development (HUD). RESPA also regulates the relationship between real estate brokers, lenders, escrow companies, and title insurers, and generally prohibits kickbacks, referral fees, or steering agreements among them.
>
> RESPA restricts the amount of advance insurance payments and property tax that a lender can impound (collect and reserve).

closing statement

> also called a *settlement statement*. A detailed accounting provided to the parties at the completion of a real estate transaction. This accounting lists all cash credits and debits to the parties and all sums paid through the escrow to third parties—such as lenders, appraisers, real estate brokers, and taxing agencies. The escrow officer handling the transaction's escrow prepares the closing statement.
>
> The sample HUD Settlement Statement (called the HUD-1 Form) is now used widely, even in some transactions where it is not required.

Figure 8.1 HUD Settlement Statement

A HUD Settlement Statement is shown on the next two pages. The top part of page one is used to identify the buyer (borrower), the seller, the lender, and the property. The main part of page one gives a summary of the buyer's transaction in the left column and a summary of the seller's transaction in the right column. Amounts due to each party and amounts paid by each party are listed here, with the net amounts shown at the bottom of the page.

Page two of the form lists the settlement charges. These include the commission to the brokers, loan and other fees, any interest or insurance premiums that the lender requires, reserves deposited with the lender, charges from the title company, recording and transfer charges, and any additional settlement charges.

A. Settlement Statement

U.S. Department of Housing and Urban Development

OMB Approval No. 2502-0265

B. Type of Loan

1. ☐ FHA	2. ☐ FmHA	3. ☐ Conv. Unins.	
4. ☐ VA	5. ☐ Conv. Ins.		

6. File Number:	7. Loan Number:	8. Mortgage Insurance Case Number:

C. Note: This form is furnished to give you a statement of actual settlement costs. Amounts paid to and by the settlement agent are shown. Items marked "(p.o.c.)" were paid outside the closing; they are shown here for informational purposes and are not included in the totals.

D. Name & Address of Borrower:	E. Name & Address of Seller:	F. Name & Address of Lender:

G. Property Location:	H. Settlement Agent:	
	Place of Settlement:	I. Settlement Date:

J. Summary of Borrower's Transaction		**K. Summary of Seller's Transaction**	
100. Gross Amount Due From Borrower		**400. Gross Amount Due To Seller**	
101. Contract sales price		401. Contract sales price	
102. Personal property		402. Personal property	
103. Settlement charges to borrower (line 1400)		403.	
104.		404.	
105.		405.	
Adjustments for items paid by seller in advance		**Adjustments for items paid by seller in advance**	
106. City/town taxes to		406. City/town taxes to	
107. County taxes to		407. County taxes to	
108. Assessments to		408. Assessments to	
109.		409.	
110.		410.	
111.		411.	
112.		412.	
120. Gross Amount Due From Borrower		**420. Gross Amount Due To Seller**	
200. Amounts Paid By Or In Behalf Of Borrower		**500. Reductions In Amount Due To Seller**	
201. Deposit or earnest money		501. Excess deposit (see instructions)	
202. Principal amount of new loan(s)		502. Settlement charges to seller (line 1400)	
203. Existing loan(s) taken subject to		503. Existing loan(s) taken subject to	
204.		504. Payoff of first mortgage loan	
205.		505. Payoff of second mortgage loan	
206.		506.	
207.		507.	
208.		508.	
209.		509.	
Adjustments for items unpaid by seller		**Adjustments for items unpaid by seller**	
210. City/town taxes to		510. City/town taxes to	
211. County taxes to		511. County taxes to	
212. Assessments to		512. Assessments to	
213.		513.	
214.		514.	
215.		515.	
216.		516.	
217.		517.	
218.		518.	
219.		519.	
220. Total Paid By/For Borrower		**520. Total Reduction Amount Due Seller**	
300. Cash At Settlement From/To Borrower		**600. Cash At Settlement To/From Seller**	
301. Gross Amount due from borrower (line 120)		601. Gross amount due to seller (line 420)	
302. Less amounts paid by/for borrower (line 220)	( )	602. Less reductions in amt. due seller (line 520)	( )
303. Cash ☐ From ☐ To Borrower		**603. Cash** ☐ To ☐ From Seller	

Section 5 of the Real Estate Settlement Procedures Act (RESPA) requires the following: • HUD must develop a Special Information Booklet to help persons borrowing money to finance the purchase of residential real estate to better understand the nature and costs of real estate settlement services; • Each lender must provide the booklet to all applicants from whom it receives or for whom it prepares a written application to borrow money to finance the purchase of residential real estate; • Lenders must prepare and distribute with the Booklet a Good Faith Estimate of the settlement costs that the borrower is likely to incur in connection with the settlement. These disclosures are mandatory.

Section 4(a) of RESPA mandates that HUD develop and prescribe this standard form to be used at the time of loan settlement to provide full disclosure of all charges imposed upon the borrower and seller. These are third party disclosures that are designed to provide the borrower with pertinent information during the settlement process in order to be a better shopper.

The Public Reporting Burden for this collection of information is estimated to average one hour per response, including the time for reviewing instructions, searching existing data sources, gathering and maintaining the data needed, and completing and reviewing the collection of information.

This agency may not collect this information, and you are not required to complete this form, unless it displays a currently valid OMB control number.

The information requested does not lend itself to confidentiality.

L. Settlement Charges

		Paid From Borrowers Funds at Settlement	Paid From Seller's Funds at Settlement
700. Total Sales/Broker's Commission based on price $ @ % =			
Division of Commission (line 700) as follows:			
701. $ to			
702. $ to			
703. Commission paid at Settlement			
704.			
800. Items Payable In Connection With Loan			
801. Loan Origination Fee %			
802. Loan Discount %			
803. Appraisal Fee to			
804. Credit Report to			
805. Lender's Inspection Fee			
806. Mortgage Insurance Application Fee to			
807. Assumption Fee			
808.			
809.			
810.			
811.			
900. Items Required By Lender To Be Paid In Advance			
901. Interest from to @$ /day			
902. Mortgage Insurance Premium for months to			
903. Hazard Insurance Premium for years to			
904. years to			
905.			
1000. Reserves Deposited With Lender			
1001. Hazard insurance months@$ per month			
1002. Mortgage insurance months@$ per month			
1003. City property taxes months@$ per month			
1004. County property taxes months@$ per month			
1005. Annual assessments months@$ per month			
1006. months@$ per month			
1007. months@$ per month			
1008. months@$ per month			
1100. Title Charges			
1101. Settlement or closing fee to			
1102. Abstract or title search to			
1103. Title examination to			
1104. Title insurance binder to			
1105. Document preparation to			
1106. Notary fees to			
1107. Attorney's fees to			
(includes above items numbers:)			
1108. Title insurance to			
(includes above items numbers:)			
1109. Lender's coverage $			
1110. Owner's coverage $			
1111.			
1112.			
1113.			
1200. Government Recording and Transfer Charges			
1201. Recording fees: Deed $; Mortgage $; Releases $			
1202. City/county tax/stamps: Deed $; Mortgage $			
1203. State tax/stamps: Deed $; Mortgage $			
1204.			
1205.			
1300. Additional Settlement Charges			
1301. Survey to			
1302. Pest inspection to			
1303.			
1304.			
1305.			
1400. Total Settlement Charges (enter on lines 103, Section J and 502, Section K)			

Use the Right Term

Circle the letter of the choice that best completes each statement. Use the definitions of the terms and your logic to determine the best answer. The answers are shown at the end of the chapter.

1. Closing costs _____.

    (a) are always paid entirely by the buyer

    (b) are always paid entirely by the seller

    (c) include the price of the property

    (d) none of the above

2. Closing costs _____.

    (a) may include prorated taxes

    (b) may include escrow fees

    (c) may include title insurance costs

    (d) all of the above

3. The allocation of costs to a buyer and a seller so that each pays his or her fair share is called _____.

    (a) a dividend

    (b) cost appraising

    (c) prorating

    (d) rent

4. A good faith estimate of closing costs _____.

    (a) is prepared by a lender for a borrower

    (b) is prepared by a seller for a buyer

    (c) does not allow for comparisons of fees

    (d) none of the above

5. A HUD Settlement Statement _____.

    (a) contains more information and detail than a good faith estimate of closing costs

    (b) is prepared for both buyer and seller of the property in question

(c) is required by law for transactions involving certain types of loans

(d) all of the above

3. Other Escrow-Related Terms

beneficiary statement
close into escrow (dry closing)
closing date

closing meeting
concurrent recording
walk-through

beneficiary statement

a statement indicating the unpaid balance on a note (loan) secured by a trust deed. When the sellers of a property still have a balance on their home loan (a note), they must provide a beneficiary statement to the escrow officer. Usually, the escrow officer will use the proceeds from the sale of the property to pay the sellers' lender for the balance due.

close into escrow (dry closing)

the signing of documents by all parties to a transaction, which documents are then held by the escrow officer or attorney pending resolution of an issue or receipt of a delayed document. Dry closings are not common, but are sometimes unavoidable due to postal and other delays. Although the documents are signed, money is not disbursed and the transaction is not recorded nor the deed delivered until the missing document arrives or the cause of the delay is resolved.

closing date

the date on which title to a property is actually transferred or recorded. This date may be a day or so after the loan monies have been submitted.

closing meeting

a meeting, more common in eastern states, at which the buyer pays for the property and receives a deed. In western states, it is more common for the escrow officer to handle the closing without a meeting with the buyer and seller by assembling all the required signed documents and monies, ordering the recordation of the title, and then sending the parties their respective payments and document copies.

concurrent recording

the closing and recording of two separate transactions simultaneously. Concurrent recordings are more often used for trades or exchanges (see Chapter 7) than for simple purchase transactions.

Using Real Estate Terms

Frank Barnes wanted to sell his house and buy Gail Carpenter's house in town. Frank found a buyer for his house, and then he and Gail agreed that when the transaction of selling Frank's house was recorded, the transaction of his buying Gail's house would record at the same time. ▲▲▲

---

walk-through

a final inspection of a property by its buyer, conducted just prior to close of escrow, to see that the condition of the property is as expected and that all required repairs have been completed.

Using Real Estate Terms

The day before his home purchase was due to close, Harry Sun and his agent completed a walk-through of the property. They discovered that in the two weeks since they had last been in the house the tenants had damaged the kitchen door and broken two windows. Since the condition had been specified in the agreement, Harry said that he wanted the sellers to repair the windows and the door before he would complete the transaction. ▲▲▲

Use the Right Term

Circle the letter of the choice that best completes each statement. Use the definitions of the terms and your logic to determine the best answer. The answers are shown at the end of the chapter.

1. Which of the following is an example of concurrent recording?

    (a) Dave has two escrows open at the same time.

    (b) Dave's home sale and George's home sale record on the same day.

    (c) As stipulated in Dave's sales contract for the purchase of his new house, the transfer of title to Dave was recorded at the same time as the transfer of title of his old house to the new owners.

    (d) Dave opens two escrows on the same day.

2. A beneficiary statement _____.

    (a) indicates the holder of a note (loan) on a property

    (b) indicates the balance due on a note (loan) on a property

    (c) is provided to the escrow officer when the property is being sold

    (d) all of the above

3. Which of the following is an example of dry closing?

    (a) An escrow closes after the title has been transferred.

    (b) An escrow closes on a property that has no river or lake shoreline.

    (c) The loan on a property is not approved.

    (d) Some aspect of a property sale transaction creates a delay, but all parties sign the documents and the transaction closes later.

4. The date on which title to a property is actually transferred or recorded is _____.

    (a) midnight December 31 of the transaction year

    (b) not important to the closing of a transaction

    (c) the closing date

    (d) the date of the closing meeting

Review & Practice: Escrow

closing costs	outside of escrow
escrow	prorating
escrow fees	RESPA
escrow instructions	settlement statement
escrow officer	walk-through

Select the term from the list above that best fits the blank in each sentence below.

1. Iris Cox bought June Steele's home. She also bought June's snow mobile, but this was _____.

2. When Iris bought June's home, she paid her fair share of the year's property taxes. This is known as _____.

3. _____ is the process of collecting and distributing the funds and documents needed to complete a real estate transaction.

4. Escrow services are performed by a neutral third party called
   _____.

5. Another name for a closing statement is a
   _____.

6. Shortly before the escrow on their house closed escrow, Kevin and Louise confirmed that the house was in the condition they expected by doing a final _____.

7. _____ requires settlement (closing) procedures and loan costs.

8. _____ include a list of the documents, funds, and other items to be placed into escrow.

9. Expenses of consummating a real estate transaction that are separate from the actual price of the property are called
   _____.

10. The amounts charged by the escrow company for the processing of a transaction are called the _____.

Short Answer

Use the space provided to answer the following questions.

1. What are the duties of an escrow officer?

2. What does the abbreviation *RESPA* stand for? What are its key features?

3. Mason George is buying Sam Norton's property. Sam leases a small storage unit to Tom Olson. Tom paid Sam $1,200, the rent on the storage unit for a full year, from January 1 through December 31. The sale of the property will close on August 31. Explain what amount of credit Mason will receive and why.

4. What is meant by *dry closing*? Give an example.

5. What is the main purpose of a good faith estimate of closing costs? Who prepares such estimates? For whom?

6. What are the main functions of an *escrow*?

7. List four assumptions that are made about the market value of a property.

8. List five examples of expenses that might be part of closing costs.

9. What is a *HUD Settlement Statement*?

10. Who prepares escrow instructions? What types of information are
    needed to prepare those instructions?

*Indicate whether each of the following statements is true or false by circling T or
F. The answers are shown at the end of the chapter.*

T F   1. Escrow instructions list fees and other expenses that will be
            shared (prorated) by the buyer and the seller.

T F   2. Escrow services are performed by a neutral third party.

T F   3. A dry closing is the final transfer of ownership of real property
            from one party to another.

T F   4. At close of escrow, the seller of a property orders the recording of
            the transfer of title.

T F   5. All of the costs of the purchase of a property, other than the price
            of the property, are called escrow fees.

T F   6. *Outside of escrow* refers to a transaction, such as a buyer's purchase of gardening equipment from the seller, that is completed separately and only after the close of escrow.

T F   7. Some expenses that are often prorated include taxes, homeowner association dues, and insurance that has been paid in advance.

T F   8. The date of escrow refers to the date on which title to a property is actually transferred or recorded.

T F   9. The inspection of a property for termites and other pests is called a walk-through.

T F   10. Concurrent recording is defined as the purchase of two properties by the same person at the same time.

Answers

Escrow Basic Terms: (1) c; (2) d; (3) a; (4) a

Escrow—Money: (1) d; (2) d; (3) d; (4) a; (5) d

Other Escrow-Related Terms: (1) c; (2) d; (3) d; (4) c

Fill-In
(1) outside of escrow; (2) prorating; (3) escrow; (4) escrow officer; (5) settlement statement; (6) walk-through; (7) RESPA; (8) escrow instructions; (9) closing costs; (10) escrow fees

True or False
(1) T; (2) T; (3) F; (4) F; (5) F; (6) F; (7) T; (8) F; (9) F; (10) F

How do you know what price to set on a property? How does a lender decide how much to loan on a particular property? How do governments establish property tax levels? All of these functions require some estimate of a property's value. An appraisal is just such an estimate. Some appraisals are simply informal guesses. Usually, however, appraisals are based on more formal, professional analyses that follow certain principles and procedures that are acceptable to lenders, governments, and others.

This chapter reviews terms related to appraisal of real estate. The terms are presented as groups according the three approaches to appraisal of property: the market approach, the cost approach, and the income approach. You will also learn the terms related to the overall appraisal process.

Do You Know These Terms?

adjusted market price	effective gross income	projected gross income
adjustments	FIRREA	reconciliation
appraisal	functional obsolescence	replacement cost
appraisal approaches	gross rent multiplier	reproduction cost
buyers' market	highest and best use	scheduled gross income
capitalize	income approach	sellers' market
CMA	incurable depreciation	square-foot method
comparables	market approach; value	subject property
correlation	approach	USPAP
cost approach	market value	vacancy allowance
curable depreciation	net operating income	valuation
depreciation	operating expenses	
economic obsolescence	physical deterioration	

1. Appraisal: Basic Terms

appraisal	valuation
subject property	highest and best use
appraisal approaches	market value

appraisal

formal estimate or opinion of a property's value.

Formal appraisals are conducted by trained professionals. An appraisal is an opinion that should be written, impartial, and conducted by an independent party, that is, someone who has no interest in the property.

The written appraisal report contains a property description and presents an analysis of the data gathered by the appraiser. An appraisal is considered valid only for a particular point in time since a property's condition, neighborhood characteristics, and the economy, all of which affect a property's value, can change at any time.

Using Real Estate Terms

Kevin Pollack wished to purchase the Front Street home of Sarah Brown. Sarah said she would sell the property for $320,000. Kevin contacted a lender to obtain a loan so he could purchase the home. Before the lender would make the loan, it ordered an appraisal of the property to make sure that the property was worth the money that Kevin wanted to borrow. The appraisal indicated the market value of the property to be $365,000, which satisfied the lender's value requirement. ▲▲▲

subject property

> the property that is being appraised.

Using Real Estate Terms

In the example of Kevin Pollack and the house on Front Street, the Front Street home is the subject property. ▲▲▲

---

appraisal approaches

> the three approaches to appraisal of property, that is, the market approach, the cost approach, and the income approach.
>
> Formal appraisals often use all three approaches to estimate the value of the subject property, and then "reconcile" the values to arrive at a final appraisal figure. Terminology related to all three approaches is covered in more detail in this chapter.

valuation

> the process of estimating the value of a property. The process is systematic and follows steps described by the Uniform Standards of Professional Appraisal Practice (USPAP).
>
> The steps in the valuation process include the following:
>
> 1. identify the property and the purpose of the valuation;
> 2. select an approach and plan the appraisal based on preliminary data;
> 3. collect data;
> 4. determine the "highest and best use" of the land as though it were vacant;
> 5. determine the "highest and best use" of the land with its improvements;
> 6. estimate the value of the land;
> 7. estimate the value of the land with its improvements;
> 8. reconcile or adjust results to arrive at a final estimate of the value;
> 9. prepare a written report of the opinion of the value.

highest and best use

> the use of a property that will give it the highest value.

Using Real Estate Terms

John Ironmonger owns a three-acre parcel of land that he plants with potatoes each year. The parcel is on a corner next to the highway. The intersection is a busy one, and neighboring lots are now developed with shopping and restaurants. John's use of his parcel for growing potatoes is not the parcel's highest and best use. ▲▲▲

---

market value

also called *fair market value*; the price that a property would probably bring in a competitive and open market. Market value is the key to most real estate transactions.

Several conditions are assumed about the market value of a property. These include the following:

1. the price could be attained without any special motivating or coercive pressures on the buyer and the seller;
2. the buyer and the seller are both knowledgeable, reasonable parties, well informed, and acting in their own best interest;
3. the price could be attained in a reasonable amount of time on the market;
4. the price could be reached without exotic financing or other arrangements.

Using Real Estate Terms

The appraisal on the Front Street property indicated that the market value of the property was only $240,000. Therefore, the lender would not make the loan to Kevin.

In a different situation, Karen and Larry accepted an offer on their house for $220,000 when similar houses were selling for more than $250,000. They needed to sell quickly and so they accepted the offer of $220,000. ▲▲▲

Use the Right Term

Circle the letter of the choice that best completes each statement. Use the definitions of the terms and your logic to determine the best answer. The answers are shown at the end of the chapter.

1. Which of the following is not a step in the process of estimating the market value of a home?

   (a) Estimate the value of the land without the house.

   (b) Collect data.

   (c) Prepare a written report.

   (d) All of these steps are part of the process.

2. In an appraisal, the property that is being appraised is referred to as _____.

   (a) the owner's property

   (b) the subject property

   (c) the object of the appraisal

   (d) the target property

3. Which of the following items is/are included in a written appraisal?

   (a) a description of the property

   (b) analysis of the data collected by the appraiser

   (c) the appraiser's estimate of market value of the property

   (d) all of these are included in a written appraisal

4. Estimating the value of residential property by comparing the sales value of similar properties is called the _____ to appraisal.

   (a) market approach

   (b) lazy approach

   (c) cost approach

   (d) backward approach

5. Which of the following is not an assumption related to market value?

   (a) The price could be attained without any special motivating or coercive pressures on the buyer and the seller.

   (b) The buyer and the seller are both knowledgeable, reasonable parties, well informed, and acting in their own best interest.

   (c) This is the maximum price ever found on the market.

   (d) The price could be reached without exotic financing or other arrangements.

2. Market Approach to Appraisal

The most common approach to estimating the value of residential property is to compare the sales of similar properties. This is called the "market approach" to appraisal. Here are terms related to this approach.

market approach   adjustments
buyers' market   adjusted market price
sellers' market   correlation
comparables   gross rent multiplier
CMA

market approach

> also called *market comparison approach*, *market data approach*, or *value approach*. This appraisal approach estimates the value of a property by analyzing the recent sales of similar properties ("comparables"). In some analyses, the prices of properties currently on the market or that have been on the market but failed to sell are also considered (see CMA).

buyers' market

> a market situation in which more properties are available than there are buyers, i.e., one with many sellers but not many buyers. When a buyers' market condition exists, the expected selling value (market value) of homes may not be as high as when a sellers' market exists.

sellers' market

> a market situation in which relatively few properties are available for sale, i.e., one with many buyers but not many sellers. When a sellers' market condition exists, the expected selling value (market value) of homes may be higher than when a buyers' market exists.

Using Real Estate Terms

The Bowertons put their residence on the market in early February. It was a well maintained home in a good neighborhood, and it was the most popular model in the tract. By July the house still had not been sold. "You might need to lower your price," their agent said. "There are many homes for sale right now, and not very many people are buying. The prices of houses have been falling fast because sellers are competing for buyers' attention. It's a buyers' market!" ▲▲▲

comparables

properties that are similar to the subject property in size, age, location, features, etc.

CMA

competitive market analysis, also sometimes called a *comparative market analysis*; a report that estimates the value of a property by examining recent sales of similar homes as well as the prices of homes currently on the market and of homes that have been on the market recently but failed to sell. A CMA is most often used for purposes of helping a client place a price on a property that is about to go on the market. Usually prepared by a real estate agent, it is more a marketing tool than a formal, "official" appraisal.

adjustments

that part of the appraisal process that increases or decreases the estimated value of a comparable to improve its equivalency to the subject property. This usually consists of adding dollars to the figure used for a comparable property for positive features that the subject property has but that the comparable does not have. Similarly, dollars are subtracted from the estimate when the comparable property has fewer features or a less desirable location, for example, than the subject property.

In other words, we want to use a value for the comparable that is closest to what it would be worth if it were exactly like the subject property. Therefore, we would add dollars for features, size, etc. that the subject property has but the comparable property does not have.

Sample Market Approach with Adjustments

Adjustment for a feature: Stanley Taylor's house is being appraised. Stanley's house is the subject property. One of the comparables used in the appraisal is the home of Bill and Betty Barnes. The Barnes house just sold for $190,000. In the analysis process, the appraiser adjusted the comparison amount for the Barnes house upward by $5,000 because it does not have a garage or carport, but the Taylor house does have a carport.

Adjustment for land feature: The Taylor property is located at the edge of a running creek. The appraiser added $4,000 to the amount being used for the Barnes house comparison because it has no special land feature.

Adjustment for time: The Barnes house sold three months ago. In that time, the property values for that area have decreased by 1 percent. Therefore, the amount used for this comparison can be decreased by 1 percent so that the estimate is closer to today's values. Subtract $1,900 from the Barnes comparable amount.

With the three adjustments so far, we have an adjusted figure for the Barnes comparable amount of $190,000 + $5,000 + $4,000 - $1,900 = $197,100.

Note that this is not the appraised value of the Taylor property. The Barnes property is only one comparable and the appraiser would use adjusted data from several properties in calculating the Taylor property value.

SAMPLE MARKET APPROACH					
Property/ Feature	**Taylor** 42 W. Creek Rd.	**Barnes** 53 W. Creek Rd.		**Easton** 28 N. Cross St.	
Sale Price	N/A	$190,000		$202,000	
Time of sale	N/A	3 months ago. Subtract 1 percent	- $1900	1 year ago. Add 5 percent	+ $10,100
Size	1600 sq. ft.	1610 sq. ft.	N/A	1800 sq. ft. Subtract $22,000	- $22,000
Garage	Carport	No garage or carport	+ $5000	Carport	--
Other	Creek	None. Add $4000	+ $4000	None. Add $4000	+ $4,000
Condition	Excellent	Excellent	--	Needs new roof.	+ $6,000
Landscaping etc.	Professional hardscape	Excellent	--	Fair. Needs work.	+ $6,000
Total Adjustment			+ $7,100		+ $4,000
Adjusted Market Price		$197,100		$206,000	

adjusted market price

> the value of a comparable property after adjustments have been added and subtracted to make it as much like the subject property as possible.

correlation

> the process of giving weights to the adjusted market values of comparables to arrive at and to improve the accuracy of an appraised value.

Sample Correlation

The appraiser has decided to give a little more weight to the Barnes property since it is on the same street as the Taylor property and therefore probably closer in value. In the correlation process depicted in the following table, notice that the Barnes property accounts for 60% of the value and the Easton property accounts for 40% of the value. The final value given for the subject property in the appraisal is $198,500.

Correlation of Comparables Data for Subject Property, 42 W. Creek Rd.			
Property	Adjusted Market Price	"Weight"	Amount toward Market Value of Subject Property
Barnes	$197,100	60%	$118,260
Easton	$206,000	40%	$ 80,240
Total Value assigned to subject property:			$198,500

▲▲▲

gross rent multiplier

> a method that permits a market approach to the valuation of an income-producing property; a number that, when multiplied by the gross rents of a property, gives an estimate of the value of that property.

Use the Right Term

Circle the letter of the choice that best completes each statement. Use the definitions of the terms and your logic to determine the best answer. The answers are shown at the end of the chapter.

1. The appraiser of Janet Evans' home found data on three homes in her neighborhood that were similar to Janet's and that had sold recently. Which of the following will be among the appraiser's next steps?

(a) Select the home with the highest price and use that price as the market value.

(b) Select the home with the lowest price and use that price as the market value.

(c) Adjust the figures for the three homes in order to make them more equivalent to Janet's property.

(d) Contact the owners of the three homes in the comparison.

2. The homes being used for comparison purposes in the previous example are referred to as _____.

   (a) comparables

   (b) comparatives

   (c) comprehensives

   (d) none of the above

3. When Dave and Georgia Graves decided to sell their house, a real estate agent gave them an analysis she had prepared. The analysis showed data on similar properties and recommended a price to ask for the property. The real estate agent's analysis was

   _____.

   (a) an appraisal

   (b) an appraisal report

   (c) a CMA

   (d) useless

4. The process of giving a certain level of importance or "weight" to the value of comparables is called _____.

   (a) skewing the data

   (b) correlation of the data

   (c) fixing the data

   (d) none of the above

Use information in the following table for the next four questions.

Correlation of Comparables Data for Subject Property, 7584 Ash St.			
Property	Adjusted Price	"Weight"	Amount toward Market Value of Subject Property
Comparable A	$297,100	20%	$ 59,420
Comparable B	$340,000	80%	$ 272,000
Total Value assigned to subject property:			$ 331,420

5. What is the address of the subject property?

6. What is the adjusted market price of Comparable A?

7. What weight (percentage) did the appraiser give Comparable A?

8. What was the appraised value given to the subject property?

9. The market approach to valuation _____.

    (a) cannot be used with income properties

    (b) uses a gross rent multiplier for income properties

    (c) is used only with income properties

    (d) none of the above

10. A gross rent multiplier _____.

    (a) is used as a market approach for income properties

    (b) is not used as a market approach for income properties

    (c) is used as a cost approach for income properties

    (d) is not a valid method for anything

3. Cost Approach to Appraisal

cost approach   economic obsolescence
replacement cost   functional obsolescence
reproduction cost   physical deterioration
square-foot method   curable depreciation
depreciation   incurable depreciation

The cost approach to appraisal examines what the subject property would cost if constructed anew. Here are some terms related to this approach.

cost approach

an approach to estimating the value of a property based on current construction costs. This approach adds together the value of the land and what the cost of construction would be today. Then any depreciation of the subject property is subtracted to reach the estimated market value.

Two types of construction cost estimation can be used: *replacement cost* or *reproduction cost*.

replacement cost

the cost for constructing a house (or other improvement) that has the same usefulness as the subject property.

Replacement cost estimates do not reproduce features of the subject property that are obsolete or unnecessary. Also, these estimates are calculated using costs of modern construction materials and techniques.

reproduction cost

the cost for constructing a house (or other improvement) that is identical to the subject property.

Reproduction cost estimates use, to the extent possible, the same materials and techniques as used in the original construction of the subject property. This approach is not as practical as the replacement cost approach. It may, however, be more appropriate in cases of properties of historical and other significance.

square-foot method

a common approach for estimating construction costs that uses the cost of recently built improvements similar to the subject property as the basis for the estimate.

Using Real Estate Terms

To conduct a cost approach analysis of John Malcolm's 1,780 square foot house, the appraiser found a house very much like John's that had just been built nearby. He learned that the newly constructed house had 2,000 square feet and had cost $154,000 to build. This calculates to be $77 per square foot. The appraiser applied this figure to the size of John's house. At $77 per square foot, the construction cost of a 1,780 square foot house would be $136,060.

This amount does not include the cost of the land, so the appraiser added $52,000, the value of John's lot, to the estimated value, arriving at a value of $188,060.

Next, the appraiser subtracted some amounts from this estimate for depreciation because John's house was in need of various repairs. ▲▲▲

depreciation

> (see also Chapter 11) a lowering in value due to age, disrepair, the economy, and other factors. Appraisers consider three types of depreciation: *physical deterioration*, *functional obsolescence*, and *economic obsolescence*. See the following entries.

economic obsolescence

> conditions or events that are external to the subject property that lead to a lessening of its value. Examples would include a drop in the demand for housing, construction of freeways, airports, or other noise-generating improvements near the property, and the deterioration and disrepair of nearby properties.

Using Real Estate Terms

Sue Ames took excellent care of her property. The home and lot were well maintained, and she had upgraded the roof, walkways, and landscaping. Sue's neighbors, however, were not as concerned about maintaining their houses, and the street in general looked run-down. Even though Susan's house looked good, the value suffered from the economic obsolescence caused by the other homes' deterioration. ▲▲▲

functional obsolescence

> old and unfashionable design and/or outdated fixtures or systems that lead to a lessening of the value of the subject property. An outdated system might include plumbing made from old materials or outdated electrical wiring. Outdated fixtures might include old bathroom and kitchen counters, cupboards, and sinks.

Using Real Estate Terms

Patrick Sullivan's older four-bedroom home had only one bathroom. It had no garage or carport and no space for adding one. The very design of the home reflected an earlier age, before homes were designed with multiple bathrooms and when garages were not considered absolutely necessary. The value of Patrick's home suffers from functional obsolescence in its design. ▶▶▶

physical deterioration

> disrepair or wear and tear on a property that leads to a lessening of its value. Examples include roof leaks, non-operational appliances, worn-out carpeting, and broken windows.

curable depreciation

> depreciation from functional or physical deterioration that can be "cured," that is, repaired or replaced, for reasonable cost. Worn carpeting, broken roof tiles, and peeling paint can all be replaced or otherwise fixed for reasonable cost.

incurable depreciation

> depreciation from functional or physical deterioration that *cannot* be "cured," that is, repaired or replaced for reasonable cost. Little can be done for reasonable cost, for example, to "cure" the functional obsolescence of a house that occupies most of its lot but has no garage.

Sample Cost Approach Summary

To arrive at a more accurate estimate of property value, the appraiser of John Malcolm's property (see example at "square-foot method") subtracted depreciation from the estimated value. The property needed a new $10,000 roof, new carpeting for $4,000, and new kitchen cabinets for $4,000, a total of $18,000 of needed repair and updating. The resulting calculations are shown in the following table.

Example of Cost Approach Summary	
for John Malcolm's 1,780 square-foot house	
Construction cost	$136,060 (add)
Land value	52,000 (add)
Subtotal	188,060
Depreciation	18,000 (subtract)
Estimated Value	$170,060

▶▶▶

Use the Right Term

Circle the letter of the choice that best completes each statement. Use the definitions of the terms and your logic to determine the best answer. The answers are shown at the end of the chapter.

1. Which of the following is an example of functional obsolescence?

   (a) a utility room without windows

   (b) dormer windows

   (c) old plumbing

   (d) flocked wallpaper

2. Which of the following is an example of economic obsolescence?

   (a) expensive landscaping

   (b) property owner loss of employment

   (c) run-down neighborhood

   (d) none of the above

3. Which of the following is an example of curable depreciation?

   (a) flocked wallpaper

   (b) ratty carpet

   (c) broken windows

   (d) all of the above

4. Which of the following is an accurate summary of an estimate of value using a cost approach method?

   (a) construction cost minus land value

   (b) construction cost minus depreciation

   (c) construction cost plus land value minus depreciation

   (d) construction cost minus land value minus depreciation

4. Income Approach to Appraisal

income approach   operating expenses
capitalize   net operating income (NOI)
projected gross income   effective gross income
scheduled gross income   vacancy allowance

income approach

> an approach to appraisal that uses an estimate of the income the property might produce in the future to calculate the present value of the property; to estimate the value of a property by "capitalizing its income stream."

capitalize

> to estimate current value of a property (or business) based on an estimate of future income.

Using Real Estate Terms

The Barnes Apartments building is expected to have $24,000 of a year's income remaining after expenses are paid. What should Investor Irwin pay for the building? This depends on what return Investor Irwin wishes to make on his investment. The formula is "estimate of income after expenses" divided by "rate of return." If Investor Irwin requires a return of 8 percent on his investment, then the price he would be willing to pay would be $24,000 divided by .08, or $300,000. ▲▲▲

---

projected gross income

> (also called *scheduled gross income*) an estimate of a property's future income based on the property's history of income (rents) and current operating expenses.

operating expenses

> the expenses required to maintain the income production of a property. Examples of such expenses include property taxes, insurance, property management, utilities, trash, gardening, repairs, and janitorial services.

net operating income (NOI)

> the effective gross income *minus* operating expenses.

effective gross income

the amount remaining after the amount attributed to expected vacancies or non-payment of rents is subtracted from the projected or scheduled gross income.

vacancy allowance

an estimate of an amount of income that will not be gained because of vacant units. A similar allowance is usually made for anticipated non-payment of rent. The vacancy allowance is subtracted from the projected (scheduled) income to arrive at an effective gross income.

Sample Statement for Use with Income Approach

Statement for Claymore Apartments		
Projected (or "Scheduled") Gross Income		$164,000
Allowance for vacancies and non-payment of rents		12,000
Effective gross income		152,000
Operating expenses		
Property taxes	14,000	
Insurance	4,000	
Property management	16,000	
Utilities	8,000	
Trash	2,400	
Gardening	3,600	
Repairs	6,000	
Janitorial services	1,200	
Total operating expenses		55,200
Net operating income		$96,800

▲▲▲

Use the Right Term

Circle the letter of the choice that best completes each statement. Use the definitions of the terms and your logic to determine the best answer. The answers are shown at the end of the chapter.

1. Property taxes and utilities are examples of _____.

   (a) projected gross operating expenses

   (b) operating expenses

   (c) net operating expenses

   (d) net operating income

2. The general formula for net operating income is _____.

   (a) projected gross income minus operating expenses

   (b) projected gross income minus vacancy adjustments minus operating expenses

   (c) effective gross income minus vacancy adjustments minus operating expenses

   (d) none of the above

3. An estimate of the income that a property should produce in the future is called _____.

   (a) net income

   (b) operating income

   (c) projected gross income

   (d) none of the above

4. Capitalizing involves estimating _____.

   (a) the current value of a property based on an estimate of its future income

   (b) the future value of a property based on an estimate of its current income

   (c) the net operating income of a property

   (d) none of these

5. Reconciling and Reporting

reconciliation   USPAP
FIRREA

reconciliation

judgment and analysis of the results of using the three (or even two) appraisal approaches in estimating the value of a property. In theory, in a world where all data is completely accurate and never conflicting, the results of the three approaches should be fairly similar. If one is very different from the other two, it may have an error in its analysis, and the appraiser will re-examine the data.

When reconciling the results of the three appraisal approaches, the appraiser decides which approach to "weight," or rely on, most heavily. For example, the results of the income approach might be more relevant for an older inner-city apartment building than the cost approach. (See earlier sections of this chapter for more information on these approaches.)

Sample Reconciliation

The Fitchett's house was built in 1922. When the appraiser reconciled the market, cost, and income approaches for this property, she gave the most weight to the market approach. See the table below.

Fitchett Property Reconciliation			
Approach	Amount	Weight	Value to apply
Market approach	$360,000	75%	$270,000
Cost approach	$600,000	15%	$90,000
Income approach	$202,000	10%	$20,200
Final (Reconciled) Value			$380,000

FIRREA

Title XI of the Financial Institution's Reform, Recovery, and Enforcement Act of 1989, which establishes standards for appraiser qualifications.

USPAP

Uniform Standards of Professional Appraisal Practice. The mandatory requirements established by FIRREA for some federally related appraisals. USPAP specifies appraisal report standards.

Use the Right Term

Circle the letter of the choice that best completes each statement. Use the definitions of the terms and your logic to determine the best answer. The answers are shown at the end of the chapter.

1. An appraiser would be most likely to give more weight to an income approach valuation for _____.

   (a) an apartment complex

   (b) a one-year-old ranch-style home

   (c) a 50-year-old residence

   (d) none of the above

2. An appraiser would be most likely to give more weight to a cost approach valuation for _____.

   (a) a court house

   (b) a bus station

   (c) a school

   (d) all of the above

3. The purpose of the reconciliation phase of an appraisal is to _____.

   (a) identify the highest possible value for the subject property

   (b) use data from the three approaches to the appropriate degree

   (c) to equalize the data from the three approaches

   (d) none of the above

4. Title XI of the Financial Institution's Reform, Recovery, and Enforcement Act of 1989 _____.

   (a) requires financial institutions to perform appraisals

   (b) is part of USPAP

   (c) establishes standards for appraiser qualifications.

   (d) all of the above

Review & Practice: Appraisal

capitalizing   income approach   reconciliation
correlation   incurable depreciation   reproduction cost
cost approach   market approach
functional obsolescence   operating expenses

Select the term from the list above that best fits the blank in each sentence below.

1. The _____ to valuation compares the value of similar properties in order to estimate the value of the subject property.

2. The county built a new high-traffic road that borders on Janet Oldham's property. As a result of the noise, the value of Janet's property has depreciated. This is an example of
_____.

3. Cara Bigger's large two-story frame house, which was built in the 1920s, has only one bathroom, which is located down the hall from the five upstairs bedrooms. This design does not meet the requirements and expectations of modern families, and would be considered an example of _____.

4. Greg and Gloria would have to pay $400,000 if they were to build a home identical to theirs at today's construction costs. This amount is called _____.

5. An approach to appraisal that relies on estimates of a property's future income as a basis for determining value is called the
_____.

6. The process of adjusting the value of comparable properties so that they more closely represent the value of a subject property is called
_____.

7. The process of applying a weight to the values determined by the three approaches to valuating a subject property in order to arrive at a final appraised value is called _____.

8. The approach to appraisal that estimates the value of a property by estimating the current construction costs for an identical or similar property is called the _____.

9. To estimate the present value of a property based on its future income is called _____.

10. The costs of maintaining a property, including taxes, insurance, repairs, and other costs, are called _____.

Short Answer

Use the space provided to answer the following questions.

1. List and briefly describe the three approaches to appraisal.

2. Define and give examples of *replacement cost* and *reproduction cost*.

3. Describe the situations called *buyers' market* and *sellers' market*.

4. Explain the difference between *curable* and *incurable obsolescence*.

5. How is a CMA different from an appraiser's market approach to valuation?

6. Describe and give an example of the square-foot method of estimating the value of a property.

7. List four assumptions made about the market value of a property.

8. Define and give examples of the *correlation* and *reconciliation* steps of the appraisal process.

9. Explain the difference between *scheduled gross income* and *net operating income*. How are they calculated?

10. What is a *vacancy allowance*?

True or False

Indicate whether each of the following statements is true or false by circling T or F. The answers are shown at the end of the chapter.

T F   1. Wear and tear on a property results in economic depreciation.

T F   2. The appraisal process follows the steps described in the United States Professional Appraisal Principles.

T F   3. Comparables are properties similar to a subject property.

T F   4. The use of a property that gives the greatest value is called its highest and best use.

T F   5. Capitalization is estimating future value based on current value.

T F   6. Depreciation is a loss in value that can be the result of either deterioration or obsolescence.

T F   7. A buyers' market is a situation that is considered advantageous for buying.

T F   8. The three appraisal approaches are the comparison, the competitive, and the cost approaches.

T F   9. Appraisers first select one approach to estimating the value of a property and then apply only that approach to reach a final appraised value.

T F   10. The net operating income of a property is the money left over after operating expenses and a deduction for a vacancy allowance.

Answers

Appraisal—Basic Terms: (1) d; (2) b; (3) c; (4) a; (5) c

Market Approach to Appraisal: (1) c; (2) a; (3) c; (4) b; (5) 7584 Ash St.; (6) $297,100; (7) 20%; (8) $331,420; (9) b; (10) a

Cost Approach to Appraisal: (1) c; (2) c; (3) d; (4) c

Income Approach to Appraisal: (1) b; (2) b; (3) c; (4) a

Reconciling and Reporting: (1) a; (2) d; (3) b; (4) c

Fill-In
(1) market approach; (2) incurable depreciation; (3) functional obsolescence; (4) reproduction cost; (5) income approach; (6) correlation; (7) reconciliation; (8) cost approach; (9) capitalizing; (10) operating expenses

True or False
(1) F; (2) F; (3) T; (4) T; (5) F; (6) T; (7) T; (8) F; (9) F; (10) T

Leases may pertain to land, residential, or commercial properties, and many of them are quite complex. What are the major types of leases? How are rents determined? What rights do lessors and lessees hold? The sections in this chapter cover terms in the following groups: leasehold estate and types of leasehold estate, lease assignment, eviction; rent, and related terms.

Do You Know These Terms?

actual eviction	gross lease	percentage lease
assignee	ground lease	periodic estate
assignment	ground rent	quiet enjoyment
assignor	holdover tenant	retaliatory eviction
constructive eviction	index lease	reversion
contract rent	leasehold estate	step-up rent
economic rent	lessee	sublease
escalator clause	lessor	sublessee
estate at will	month-to-month lease	sublessor
estate for years	net lease, triple net lease	sublet
eviction	option clause	tenancy at sufferance
graduated rent	participation clause	

1. Leasehold Estate

leasehold estate   lessor
lessee

leasehold estate

the right that a tenant has to occupy land and its buildings,
usually in return for paying rent to the owner of the property. A
leasehold estate could be an *estate for years* or a *periodic estate*.
(See related terms in the next section.)

lessee

the person or entity who has the right to occupy another person's
property by reason of a lease, usually in return for paying rent. A
lessee may commonly be referred to as the *tenant* or the *renter*.

lessor

a person or entity who has given the right to another to occupy his
or her land and its buildings, usually in return for rent. A lessor is
the owner of the property and may commonly be referred to as the
landlord.

Using Real Estate Terms

Turner Wainwright owns a colonial style house on Witness Creek, which he
rents out to Henry and Clara Jane Sample. Turner Wainwright has the right
to collect rent from the Samples, and the Samples have the right to occupy
the property. The Samples hold a leasehold estate on the property. They
are the lessees. Turner Wainwright is referred to as the lessor. ▶▶▶

Use the Right Term

*Circle the letter of the choice that best completes each statement. Use the
definitions of the terms and your logic to determine the best answer. The answers
are shown at the end of the chapter.*

1. Sally and Joe Kellam rent their home from Tom Matthews. Which of
    the following is true?

    (a) Sally and Joe do not have any rights to the home.

    (b) Sally and Joe own the property for as long as they live there.

    (c) Sally and Joe have the right to occupy the home.

    (d) Tom Matthews is a scoundrel.

2. Tom Matthews is called the _____.

    (a) leaseholder

    (b) lessee

    (c) lessor

    (d) renter

3. Tom Matthews also leases a house to the Moores. Tom Matthews _____.

    (a) has no rights to either property

    (b) has the right to collect rent on only one property

    (c) has the right to collect rents on both properties

    (d) none of the above

4. In this situation, the Moores and the Kellams are not _____.

    (a) leaseholders

    (b) lessees

    (c) lessors

    (d) renters

2. Types of Leasehold Estate

estate for years   periodic estate
estate at will   reversion
holdover tenant   tenancy at sufferance
month-to-month lease

estate for years

a lease that has a specific starting date and ending date. An estate for years may be for any period of time, including a period of less than one year. An estate for years is not automatically renewed.

Using Real Estate Terms

Bill and Rebecca Bunting leased their property from March 16, 20XX to September 16 of the same year. Although the lease was only for six months, it was still an estate for years. ▲▲▲

---

estate at will

> a lease that can be terminated at any time by either the tenant or the landlord. An estate at will is not a common type of lease.

Using Real Estate Terms

Sue and Jim Core rent their home from Russell Smaw. Sue and Jim expect Jim's mother to come live with them at some point in the next year, at which time they will need a larger place. The Cores and Russell Smaw agreed that they would continue to rent this home until such time as Jim's mother sells her house and comes to live with them. ▲▲▲

---

holdover tenant

> a tenant whose legal occupation of a property has expired, but who continues to occupy the premises without consent of the landlord. A holdover tenant is not much different from a trespasser—except that the holdover tenant was originally a legal occupant of the property. A landlord may evict a holdover tenant without advance notice.

Using Real Estate Terms

Lee Gray was paying rent to Jessie Dunton for the small house he lived in. The lease expired several months ago. Lee was supposed to move out at the end of the lease period, but for some reason, Lee decided not too. Lee is a holdover tenant, and Jessie may evict him without notice. ▲▲▲

---

month-to-month lease

> a type of periodic estate; a lease that renews repeatedly, one month at a time, until the tenant or landlord terminates it.

periodic estate

> a lease that renews repeatedly, for equal periods, until the tenant or landlord terminates it. A month-to-month lease is an example of a periodic estate.

Using Real Estate Terms

Jane Lewis has a month-to-month lease on Abel Irvin's farmhouse. This is an example of a periodic estate. The lease renews each month for another one-month period. Either Jane or Abel can terminate the lease. ▲▲▲

reversion

the right held by a landlord to take possession of a property at the end of a lease period.

Using Real Estate Terms

Harold Reynolds leases his two-story colonial house to the Pickett family. The lease expires on August 15. At that time, if Harold and the Picketts do not decide to renew the lease, Harold has the right to take possession of the house. This right is known as reversion. ▲▲▲

---

tenancy at sufferance

tenancy that occurs when a tenant, without consent of the landlord, continues to occupy a property after the lease has ended.

Using Real Estate Terms

When his lease expired several months ago. Lee was supposed to move out, but he decided not too. He continued to occupy the property without the owner's consent. This situation is called tenancy at sufferance. ▲▲▲

Use the Right Term

Circle the letter of the choice that best completes each statement. Use the definitions of the terms and your logic to determine the best answer. The answers are shown at the end of the chapter.

1. Shirley and Jake Collins rent their home from Sally Custis. They have a lease that began on November 1 of last year and that ends on May 17. Shirley and Jack have _____.

   (a) a tenancy at sufferance

   (b) an estate at sufferance

   (c) periodic tenancy

   (d) an estate for years

2. Sally Custis has the right to take possession of her property at the end of the lease. This right is called _____.

   (a) repossession

   (b) reversion

   (c) retaking estate

   (d) resolution

3. A month-to-month lease is an example of _____.

    (a) a periodic estate

    (b) a reversion

    (c) an estate at will

    (d) an estate for years

4. An estate at will _____.

    (a) is the most common type of lease

    (b) can be terminated at any time by either the lessee or the lessor

    (c) is a property bequeathed to another party

    (d) is a periodic estate

3. Lease Assignment

assignment	sublease
assignee	sublessee
assignor	sublessor
sublet	

assignment

transfer of all of the leasehold rights held by a lessee to another person or entity.

assignee

the person or entity who receives the leasehold rights from the lessee by virtue of an assignment.

assignor

the lessee whose rights are transferred to another person or entity by virtue of an assignment.

Using Real Estate Terms

Tina Shore signed a one-year lease on Gina Northam's house. After she had lived there for a few months, her company transferred her to work in a different town. Tina's friend Sue Padilla said that she would like to rent the house for the remainder of the lease. Gina Northam, the owner, agreed that the lease and the rights and responsibilities that it represented could be transferred to Sue. This transfer is an assignment. Tina is the assignor, because the rights being assigned to Sue belonged to Tina. Sue is the assignee because she is receiving the rights that Tina had. ▲▲▲

sublet

> transfer of part of the leasehold rights held by a lessee to another person or entity. This could be rights to just a portion of the property or a portion of the time period of the lease. The sublessee pays the rent for the subleased portion to the original lessee, who pays all the rent to the landlord (lessor).

sublease

> a lease giving partial leasehold rights from a lessee to a sublessee.

sublessee

> the person or entity who receives the partial leasehold rights from the lessee by virtue of a sublease.

sublessor

> the lessee, part of whose rights are transferred to another person or entity by virtue of a sublease.

Using Real Estate Terms

Riley and Jane Pickett leased Pine Coast Farm from Tim Sandoval. In addition to the big farmhouse, the property had a guesthouse, a barn, and some other buildings. Riley and Jane decided to rent the guesthouse to Polly Tazewell. This arrangement was a sublease. The Picketts were the sublessors, and Polly Tazewell was the sublessee. Polly paid rent to the Picketts for the guesthouse, and the Picketts paid rent to Tim Sandoval for the whole farm.

▶▶▶

Use the Right Term

Circle the letter of the choice that best completes each statement. Use the definitions of the terms and your logic to determine the best answer. The answers are shown at the end of the chapter.

1. The transfer of all the rights of a lease from the lessee to another person or entity is called _____.

    (a) a tenancy at sufferance

    (b) an estate lease

    (c) an assignment

    (d) a sublease

2. An assignor is _____.

    (a) the original lessor

    (b) the original lessee

    (c) the assignee

    (d) the property owner

3. The transfer of a portion of the rights of a lease from the lessee to another person or entity is called _____.

    (a) a tenancy at sufferance

    (b) an estate lease

    (c) an assignment

    (d) a sublease

4. A sublessee _____.

    (a) leases a portion of a property from a property owner

    (b) has partial rights to a property from a sublessor

    (c) pays rent to the original lessor

    (d) none of the above

4. Eviction

eviction   constructive eviction
actual eviction   retaliatory eviction

eviction

the legal process of removing a tenant from a property.

actual eviction

the legal process of removing a tenant from a property for breaking the terms of a lease agreement. Actions that break lease terms include, for example, nonpayment of rent, holding over past the lease term, occupying a property with more persons than allowed by the lease, bringing animals into a "no pets" property, or conducting illegal activities on the property.

The steps of the process include the following:

- The landlord has notice served on the tenant that orders the tenant to comply with the terms of the lease or to move out.

- If the tenant does not comply with the terms and does not move out, the landlord goes to court.
- If the landlord wins the case in court, the court terminates the tenant's lease rights, and a marshal or sheriff goes to the property and forces the tenant to leave.

constructive eviction

the type of eviction that occurs when a landlord does not keep the property fit for occupancy by the tenant.

Using Real Estate Terms

Ralph Widgeon asked his landlord to fix the heating time and again, but the landlord refused to get it repaired. Finally Ralph moved out. This is an example of constructive eviction. Ralph might claim wrongful eviction or sue the landlord for breach of contract to try to make the landlord fix the heating. ▲▲▲

---

retaliatory eviction

an illegal type of eviction that occurs when a landlord evicts a tenant in response to the tenant's complaint.

Using Real Estate Terms

When her landlord refused to fix the plumbing and a large pool of stagnant water collected under the house, Susan Taylor reported her landlord to public health officials. Susan's action angered the landlord, who then raised her rent to get even. The landlord's action is an example of retaliatory eviction, and is illegal. ▲▲▲

Use the Right Term

Circle the letter of the choice that best completes each statement. Use the definitions of the terms and your logic to determine the best answer. The answers are shown at the end of the chapter.

1. The type of eviction that occurs when a landlord does not keep the property fit for occupancy by the tenant is called _____.

   (a) retaliatory eviction

   (b) eviction at sufferance

   (c) eviction by default

   (d) constructive eviction

2. Which of the following types of eviction is illegal?

    (a) constructive eviction

    (b) actual eviction

    (c) retaliatory eviction

    (d) lessor eviction

3. Which of the following happens in the process of an actual eviction?

    (a) The landlord has notice served on the tenant that orders the tenant to comply with the terms of the lease or to move out.

    (b) If the tenant does not comply with the terms and does not move out, the landlord goes to court.

    (c) If the landlord wins the case in court, the court terminates the tenant's lease rights, and a marshal or sheriff goes to the property and forces the tenant to leave.

    (d) All of the above.

4. When a landlord evicts a tenant in response to the tenant's complaint, the eviction is _____.

    (a) illegal eviction

    (b) retaliatory eviction

    (c) non-constructive eviction

    (d) all of the above

5. Rent

gross lease   index lease
escalator clause   net lease, triple net lease
graduated rent   percentage lease

gross lease

the type of lease in which the tenant pays a fixed amount of rent and the landlord pays the operating expenses of the property. This is the most common form of lease.

escalator clause

sometimes called a *participation clause*; a clause in a lease that allows the landlord to increase a tenant's rent to pay for increases in property taxes, utilities, maintenance, etc.

graduated rent

> also called *step-up*; the type of lease in which the rent increases over time.

index lease

> the type of lease in which the amount of rent is tied to some economic indicator, such as a cost of living index or an inflation index. Often used with office and industrial leases of five years or longer.

net lease, triple net lease

> the type of lease in which the tenant pays a base rent plus the property taxes, insurance, utilities, repairs, etc. Often used with office and industrial leases of five years or longer when an entire building is being leased.

percentage lease

> type of commercial lease in which the owner receives a percentage of the tenant's gross receipts (sales dollars) as rent or partial rent.

Using Real Estate Terms

Joan Townsend leases 100 acres of farmland from Bill Latimer. According to the terms of the lease, Joan gives Bill 20 percent of the value of her crops when she sells them. Joan has a percentage lease.

► ► ►

Art Hunter runs a small printing business in a corner shopping mall shop that he leases from Ann Suarez. He pays Ann $800 per month plus 1 percent of his total gross sales (the amount of money he collects for print jobs). Art has a percentage lease. ▲▲▲

Use the Right Term

Circle the letter of the choice that best completes each statement. Use the definitions of the terms and your logic to determine the best answer. The answers are shown at the end of the chapter.

1. The type of lease in which the rent increases over time is called

    _____.

    (a) an index lease

    (b) a graduated lease

(c) a percentage lease

(d) a net lease

2. An escalator clause _____.

   (a) allows the landlord to increase a tenant's rent to pay for increases in property taxes or other expenses subject to increases

   (b) pertains only to commercial leases of buildings with escalators

   (c) allows tenants to increase the amount of space they are renting for the same amount of rent

   (d) none of the above

3. George Ramsay pays his landlord $720 per month plus 3 percent of the money his business takes in. This arrangement is called

   _____.

   (a) an index lease

   (b) a graduated lease

   (c) a percentage lease

   (d) illegal

4. The most common form of lease is a _____.

   (a) net lease

   (b) percentage lease

   (c) graduated lease

   (d) gross lease

6. Related Terms

contract rent	ground rent
economic rent	option clause
ground lease	quiet enjoyment

contract rent

   the amount of rent that a tenant pays the landlord.

economic rent

   the amount that a property could rent for on the open market.

Using Real Estate Terms

John Lee has been leasing his office building from ABC Company for four years. He has a five-year lease (contract). He pays ABC $2,800 per month, which is the contract rent. Since John signed the lease, rents of office space in his area have increased significantly. Similar space in the building next door now rents for $4,000. ABC Company believes that this is what John's space would rent for now also. $4,000 is the approximate economic rent. ▲▲▲

ground lease

a lease of ground without lease of any buildings on the ground. This type of lease is most common for industrial and commercial properties, such as office buildings, and warehouses. The lessee leases the ground and builds (and owns) the buildings. A ground lease is most often a long-term lease of 25 to 100 years. A few areas have ground leases for residential developments, such as in Orange County, California. Problems, however, tend to develop when the ground lease expires.

ground rent

the amount of rent paid on a ground lease. The ground rent is usually a net lease and/or graduated lease.

option clause

a clause that gives a tenant the opportunity to extend or renew the lease at some stated amount of rent. (See also *lease with option to buy*, in Chapter 7.)

Using Real Estate Terms

Bill Garza rented his small office from E.B. Hunter. He signed a one-year lease with an option to renew for two additional years with a small increase in the rent. This arrangement gave Bill the flexibility to continue to occupy the office if his business succeeded or to leave the situation if the business did not do well. ▲▲▲

quiet enjoyment

the right that a tenant has to occupy and use a property without disturbance by others.

Use the Right Term

Circle the letter of the choice that best completes each statement. Use the definitions of the terms and your logic to determine the best answer. The answers are shown at the end of the chapter.

1. The amount of rent that a tenant pays the landlord is called
   _____.

   (a) index rent

   (b) contract rent

   (c) economic rent

   (d) optional rent

2. A ground lease _____.

   (a) is for ground only

   (b) allows the landlord to increase a tenant's rent to pay for increases in property taxes or other expenses subject to increases

   (c) pertains only to residential properties in Orange County, California

   (d) is usually for a term of two to five years

3. Joe and Elizabeth Irvin started a small tax services businesses. They signed a lease on an office that gave them the opportunity to extend their occupancy if their business succeeded. Their lease had
   _____.

   (a) an option clause

   (b) a long term

   (c) low rent

   (d) a flexibility warranty

4. Henry Garza pays $5,200 per month to rent the ground that his office building sits on. This rent is _____.

   (a) the ground rent

   (b) the contract rent

   (c) both the ground rent and the contract rent

   (d) the economic rent

Review & Practice: Leases

assignment	lessee
contract rent	option clause
estate for years	periodic estate
ground lease	retaliatory eviction
leasehold estate	sublease

Select the term from the list above that best fits the blank in each sentence below.

1. A _____ gives partial leasehold rights from a lessee to a sublessee.

2. Sandra Ng has a month-to-month lease on her apartment. This is an example of _____.

3. When Charles Andrews complained to the public health office about the conditions of the apartment building where he lived, the landlord raised his rent. The rent increase was a form of

   _____.

4. Doris and David Blanco turned over all their lease rights to the Stevensons. This is known as _____.

5. A person who pays rent in return for the right to occupy a property according to the terms of a lease is called the _____.

6. Harry Thomas leases space for his shop from Yolanda Evans. At the end of his lease, Harry can renew his rental for two years at the same rate. Harry's lease has an _____.

7. A lease of ground that does not include lease of buildings on the ground is called a _____.

8. The right that a tenant has to occupy land and its buildings in return for paying rent to the owner is called _____.

9. The actual rent that a lessee pays to the lessor is called

   _____.

10. Stephen Castillo holds a lease on the house where he lives. The term of the lease is March 17 through January 1 of the following year. The lease is an _____.

Short Answer

Use the space provided to answer the following questions.

1. What is the difference between *actual eviction* and *constructive eviction*?

2. Define and give an example of an *assignment*.

3. List the steps followed to carry out an *actual eviction*.

4. List four types of *leasehold estates*.

5. Explain the difference between a *lessee* and a *lessor*.

6. What is the difference between an *assignment* and a *sublease*?

7. What is a *tenancy at sufferance*? Give an example.

8. Define *contract rent* and *economic rent*.

9. Give an example of an *option clause*.

10. Explain the difference between *periodic estate* and *estate at will*. Give examples.

True or False

Indicate whether each of the following statements is true or false by circling T or F. The answers are shown at the end of the chapter.

T F 1. A month-to-month lease is a form of estate at will.

T F 2. A reversion is a tenant's right to occupy leased property.

T F 3. A holdover tenant does not have consent to continue to occupy a property.

T F 4. A sublessee has only partial lease rights to a property.

T F 5. An assignee has only partial lease rights to a property.

T F 6. Eviction that occurs when a landlord does not maintain a property is called constructive eviction.

T F 7. Economic rent is always equal to contract rent.

T F 8. Graduated rent is a hedge against inflation for the property owner.

T F 9. A lease in which the tenant pays fixed rent and the landlord pays operating expenses is a net lease.

T F 10. With a percentage lease, the lessee pays a portion of the business income as rent.

Answers

Leasehold Estate: (1) c; (2) c; (3) c; (4) c

Types of Leasehold Estate: (1) d; (2) b; (3) a; (4) b

Lease Assignment: (1) c; (2) b; (3) d; (4) b

Eviction: (1) d; (2) c; (3) d; (4) b

Rent: (1) a; (2) a; (3) c; (4) d

Related Terms: (1) c; (2) a; (3) a; (4) c

Fill-In
(1) sublease; (2) periodic estate; (3) retaliatory eviction; (4) assignment; (5) lessee; (6) option clause; (7) ground lease; (8) leasehold estate; (9) contract rent; (10) estate for years

True or False
(1) F; (2) F; (3) T; (4) T; (5) F; (6) T; (7) F; (8) T; (9) T; (10) T

Working in the world of real estate without an understanding of basic real estate finance terminology is impossible. This chapter will help you review the language of real estate finance. For practice with the math, however, you'll need to turn to a more complete text on real estate finance or real estate math.

Do You Know These Terms?

amortization	depreciation	net profit
amortization table	equity	note
Annual Percentage Rate (APR)	gross income	principal
appreciation	instrument	rate
borrower	interest	simple interest
cash flow	maturity	sweat equity
compound interest	negative cash flow	term
creditor	net income	usury

1. Changing Value

appreciation   equity
depreciation   sweat equity

The value of a property changes over time due to various factors. Characteristics such as the age and condition of the home and surrounding area, upgrades and additions, and external factors such as inflation and the overall economy, affect a property's value. Likewise, the amount of money that an owner can have left if he or she sells it and pays its mortgage balance and any other debts changes over time. Here are some terms related to these changes.

appreciation

> increase in value. Appreciation of a property results from an increase in demand for housing, a decrease in the value of money, and other factors.

Using Real Estate Terms

Andrew and Estelle Mason bought their home ten years ago for $96,000. Today they estimate that they could sell the house for $148,000. Their house has appreciated. The estimated amount of appreciation is $52,000. ▲▲▲

depreciation

> decrease in value. Depreciation of a property results from damage and wear and tear, lack of repair and maintenance, rising crime rates in a neighborhood, increase in the value of money, and other factors.

Using Real Estate Terms

Al and Elizabeth Fitchett bought their house four years ago for $220,000. Two years ago construction began on a new freeway placed one block away. When the Fitchetts tried to sell their house, they found that they could not get more than $160,000 because the freeway noise had made their home less desirable. Their house had depreciated in value. The amount of depreciation was $60,000. ▲▲▲

equity

> the part of the value of a property that is the owner's actual share; the amount of money an owner would clear after paying the mortgage balance and any other debts on the property.

Using Real Estate Terms

Today Philip and Hannah Chang can sell their house for $260,000. They still owe $180,000 on the mortgage. The estimate of their equity is the amount they will have remaining after they pay the debt on the house, that is, $260,000 minus $180,000 or $80,000. ▲▲▲

---

sweat equity

> the value that is added to a property by virtue of the owner's manual labor.

Using Real Estate Terms

After Betty Clay bought her first house, she worked every weekend remodeling the kitchen, adding ceramic tile to the bathroom, repairing the doors and windows, adding wallpaper, and landscaping the yards. As a result of her work, Betty added $30,000 to the value of the house. This $30,000 is considered sweat equity. ▲▲▲

Use the Right Term

Circle the letter of the choice that best completes each statement. Use the definitions of the terms and your logic to determine the best answer. The answers are shown at the end of the chapter.

1. An increase in value is called _____.

   (a) appreciation

   (b) depreciation

   (c) equity

   (d) none of the above

2. George Yee's gas station was successful until the new highway was constructed that did not have convenient exits. As a consequence, business dropped off and the value of the gas station decreased substantially. This is an example of _____.

(a) appreciation

(b) depreciation

(c) equity

(d) none of the above

3. Using the same example, which of the following is true?

(a) George should increase his sweat equity.

(b) Now George probably cannot sell his gas station for as much as he could have before the new highway was built.

(c) The gas station is worth more now because more cars go by on the highway.

(d) None of the above.

4. Ed Martin and his son Mike spent the summer building a new deck for the house. The materials cost very little, but it is just as nice as the neighbor's deck, which cost $8,000. Which of the following is likely to be true?

(a) This is an example of sweat equity.

(b) The Martins' equity in the house has increased.

(c) The property has appreciated as a result of having a nice deck.

(d) All of the above.

2. Borrowing

borrower	maturity
creditor	note
instrument	term

Most homebuyers borrow money to purchase their residences. Here are some basic terms related to borrowing money.

borrower

an individual or entity using someone else's money, by permission of the owner of the money and with an obligation to return the money at some future date; a debtor.

creditor

> the person or entity to whom the borrower owes the money (the debt); the lender.

instrument

> general term for a document that is prepared for legal purposes such as a will, deed, note, or contract.

maturity

> the date on which a loan is due to be repaid in full.

note

> a document detailing the amount and terms of a loan. The note is signed by the borrower and the creditor.

term

> the length of time that a borrower has to repay a loan.

Using Real Estate Terms

George and Linda Jacobs borrowed $97,000 from Alva Finance Company to put toward the purchase of their home. They signed the note on February 26, 2000. The note specified that they would repay all the money no later than February 26, 2005. In this example, Alva Finance Company is the creditor, George and Linda are the borrowers, the maturity date of the note is February 26, 2005, and the term is five years.

▲▲▲

Use the Right Term

Circle the letter of the choice that best completes each statement. Use the definitions of the terms and your logic to determine the best answer. The answers are shown at the end of the chapter.

1. A note is an example of _____.

   (a) a deed

   (b) an instrument

   (c) a period of time

   (d) a creditor

2. Maturity is _____.

    (a) the same as term

    (b) a date

    (c) a length of time

    (d) a document

3. Sophia Batson loaned Ricardo Jones $5,000. Sophia is
   _____.

    (a) a borrower

    (b) a landlord

    (c) a creditor

    (d) a bank

4. The _____ of Sophia's loan to Ricardo is three years.

    (a) maturity

    (b) date

    (c) period

    (d) term

3. Cost of Borrowing

interest	Annual Percentage Rate (APR)
simple interest	amortization
compound interest	amortization table
principal	usury
rate	

Usually we pay some amount of money for the privilege of borrowing money from someone else. The amount paid for this privilege is most often some percentage of the original amount that was borrowed. This section reviews some of the basic words and phrases related to the cost of borrowing money.

interest

payment for the use of someone else's money. The dollar amount of interest is usually calculated as a percentage of the amount of money borrowed. Two common ways to calculate interest are *simple interest* and *compound interest*.

simple interest

interest that is paid only on the money that is borrowed. Simple interest is calculated over the course of one year, without "compounding." (See *compound interest*.)

Using Real Estate Terms

Frances Parsons loaned $1,000 to her nephew, Peter. They agreed that Peter would pay back the $1,000 in one year, with 8 percent simple interest. The interest will be $80.00. This amount is 8 percent of the amount of the loan. This is an example of simple interest. ▲▲▲

---

compound interest

interest that is paid on money that is borrowed *plus* any interest that has accumulated on that money.

Using Real Estate Terms

Frances deposited $1,000 in a savings account at a local bank. Think of Frances as loaning this money to the bank. The bank is going to pay Frances interest on this money. If Frances leaves the interest in the account, now she is loaning more money to the bank. So the bank is going to pay interest on the original deposit (loan) of $1,000 plus interest on all the interest that accumulates. This is an example of compound interest. ▲▲▲

---

principal

the amount owed.

rate

the percent that is used to calculate the interest.

Annual Percentage Rate (APR)

the ratio, expressed as a percent, of all the interest and finance charges that will be paid on a loan to the total amount that is financed. The APR, which allows for comparison of loans, is required by the Federal Truth-in-Lending Act.

amortization

> payment of a loan in amounts that include some interest and some principal in each payment. As each payment is made, the amount that goes toward the principal increases and the amount that goes toward interest decreases. (This is because the rate of interest is applied only to the amount owed. As the principal amount [balance due] goes down, the interest on it is less. For example, 10 percent interest on $24,600 is less than 10 percent interest on $25,000.)

Sample Payment Table				
Payment #	Payment Amount	Part that is Principal	Part that is Interest	Balance Due on Loan
a	222.92	132.92	90.00	867.08
b	222.92	144.88	78.04	722.20
c	222.92	157.92	65.00	564.27

amortization table

> a table showing the amount of a loan payment, for a specific principal and rate and term, including both the part that goes toward the principal and the part that goes toward interest.

Sample Amortization Table Original Loan Amount: $10,000			
Interest Rate per year	10-year loan	20-year loan	30-year loan
5%	$100.61	$60.60	$53.70
6%	$111.10	$71.70	$60.00
7%	$116.20	$77.60	$66.60
8%	$121.40	$83.70	$73.40
9%	$126.70	$90.00	$80.50

usury

> charging an interest rate that is higher than the law allows.

Use the Right Term

Circle the letter of the choice that best completes each statement. Use the definitions of the terms and your logic to determine the best answer. The answers are shown at the end of the chapter.

1. Theresa Scurzzo loaned $10,000 to her daughter, Petra. They agreed that Petra would pay back the $10,000 in one year. The interest will be 7 percent of the amount of the loan, or $700. This is an example of _____.

    (a) usury

    (b) amortization

    (c) simple interest

    (d) compound interest

2. Interest is _____.

    (a) money paid for borrowing money

    (b) illegal

    (c) the amount of money borrowed

    (d) the amount of money loaned

3. Principal is _____.

    (a) the amount of money loaned

    (b) the amount of money a borrower pays interest on

    (c) the amount of money borrowed

    (d) all of the above

4. Rate is _____.

    (a) the speed or timeline for payments on a loan

    (b) the percent used to calculate interest on a loan

    (c) the percent used to compare loans

    (d) amortization

5. Amortization is _____.

    (a) loan payments that include only principal

(b) loan payments that include only interest

(c) loan payments that include only rate

(d) loan payments that include principal and interest

6. Annual Percentage Rate (APR) _____.

(a) includes consideration of interest and all the finance charges so
that a consumer can really see the total percentage being paid for
a loan

(b) allows consumers to compare what they would really pay for one
loan with what they would really pay for another loan

(c) is required by the federal Truth-in-Lending Act to help consumers
avoid hidden costs in borrowing

(d) all of these

4. Income Property

cash flow	negative cash flow
gross income	net profit

*Some finance terms in real estate apply primarily to the amounts of money
that are received or paid out by income properties. Four basic real estate
finance terms are covered in this section.*

cash flow

the amount of money remaining from the income on an investment
each year after operating expenses and mortgage payments are
paid. Note that cash flow does not consider depreciation or income
taxes. (Sometimes the phrase "cash flow" is used in the more
general sense of all the money that comes into and goes out of a
business. Here, however, we are presenting a more specific use of
the phrase.)

Using Real Estate Terms

Carrie Sykes owns a six-unit apartment building on North Creek. She receives
$60,000 each year in rent. Her operating expenses are $15,000 per year, and she
makes mortgage payments of $25,000 for the year. Her cash flow looks like this:

Rent received:	$60,000
Operating expenses	-15,000
Mortgage payments	-25,000
Cash flow	$20,000

▲▲▲

gross income

in real estate, the amount of money received from an "income-producing" property. Gross income is the total income and does not take into account expenses, taxes, depreciation, or other adjustments or deductions.

Using Real Estate Terms

Carrie Sykes receives $60,000 each year in rent on the apartment building she owns. This amount is considered her gross income. ▴▴▴

---

negative cash flow

cash flow that results when the operating expenses and mortgage payments exceeds the gross income. Owners of properties with negative cash flow must pay for some of the operating expenses and mortgage from other sources.

Using Real Estate Terms

Daniel Godwin owns a duplex from which he receives $12,000 per year in rent. Operating expenses on the duplex are $1,200 per year. Daniel pays $15,000 per year in loan payments. Cash flow on this property looks like this:

Rent received:	$12,000
Operating expenses	-1,200
Mortgage payments	-15,000
Cash flow	-$4,200

▴▴▴

---

net profit

net profit is similar to cash flow, but it does consider depreciation and does not deduct for loan payments.

Using Real Estate Terms

The net profit for Carrie Sykes' apartment building might look like this:

Rent received:	$60,000
Operating expenses	-15,000
Depreciation:	-4,000
Net Profit	$41,000

▴▴▴

Use the Right Term

Circle the letter of the choice that best completes each statement. Use the definitions of the terms and your logic to determine the best answer. The answers are shown at the end of the chapter.

1. *Cash flow* is the money left over from rent or other income after the owner pays the _____.

    (a) operating expenses

    (b) operating expenses and taxes

    (c) operating expenses and mortgage payments

    (d) mortgage payments and taxes

2. *Net profit* is the money left over from rent or other income after the owner pays the _____.

    (a) operating expenses and taxes

    (b) operating expenses and depreciation

    (c) depreciation and taxes

    (d) operating expenses and mortgage payments

3. Eddie Franks owns an alfalfa farm. Last year he received $96,000 from the sale of his alfalfa. The expenses for operating the farm last year totaled $36,000. Eddie makes mortgage payments on the farm of $8,000 for the year. Last year he figured the depreciation on the barn and equipment was $6,000. Eddie's cash flow was

    _____.

    (a) $96,000

    (b) negative

    (c) $52,000

    (d) $46,000

4. Using the same example, what was Eddie's gross income?

    (a) $36,000

    (b) $96,000

    (c) $52,000

    (d) $102,000

5. Using the same example, what was Eddie's net profit?

   (a) $54,000

   (b) $96,000

   (c) $52,000

   (d) $10,000

6. Two years ago, Eddie's fields flooded. Much of his alfalfa was ruined. When he sold it, he received only $36,000. What was Eddie's cash flow for that year? (Use the other data from item number 3.)

   (a) $96,000

   (b) negative

   (c) $52,000

   (d) $46,000

Review & Practice: Finance

amortization	maturity
cash flow	negative cash flow
compound interest	principal
creditor	simple interest
instrument	sweat equity

Select the term from the list above that best fits the blank in each sentence below.

1. The expenses and mortgage on George's triplex amounted to more than he collected in rent from the tenants. This is an example of

   _____.

2. Harry improved the value of his property by restoring the antique moldings and door/window hardware throughout the house. This is an example of _____.

3. When interest is paid on the principal of a deposit (loan) and on the interest that the deposit has already earned, it is called

   _____.

4. A _____ is the person or entity to whom money is owed.

5. Payment on a mortgage in amounts that include some interest and some principal is known as _____.

6. Jane and John Heath must have their entire loan paid on August 15 of next year. That date is known as the _____ date.

7. Income minus operating expenses and mortgage payments is called _____.

8. A note is an example of a/an _____.

9. A percentage of an original loan amount, paid in return for borrowing the money, is called _____.

10. The amount borrowed is called _____.

Short Answer

Use the space provided to answer the following questions.

1. What is the difference between *cash flow* and *negative cash flow*?

2. What is the difference between *cash flow* and *net profit*?

3. Define *Annual Percentage Rate (APR)* and explain why it is important to consumers.

4. Explain the difference between *depreciation* and *appreciation*. Give examples.

5. What is *equity*?

6. Explain the difference between *gross income* and *net profit*.

7. Explain the difference between *simple interest* and *compound interest*.

8. What is an *instrument*?

9. Explain the difference between *maturity* and *term of a loan*.

10. What is *usury*?

True or False

Indicate whether each of the following statements is true or false by circling T or F. The answers are shown at the end of the chapter.

T F 1. A borrower is a creditor.

T F 2. Amortization is a principal-only payment.

T F 3. A property can appreciate in value by virtue of a decrease in the value of a dollar.

T F 4. Simple interest is a type of compound interest.

T F 5. Amortization includes principal and interest together.

T F 6. In paying an amortized loan, over time the total amount of the principal owed is reduced.

T F 7. In paying an amortized loan, the amount of each payment that goes toward paying the principal goes up each month.

T F   8. Usury is defined as the use of another person's money.

T F   9. A borrower is defined as a person or entity that uses another person's money.

T F 10. Sweat equity can contribute to the appreciation of a property.

Answers

Changing Value: (1) a; (2) b; (3) b; (4) d

Borrowing: (1) b; (2) b; (3) c; (4) d

Cost of Borrowing: (1) c; (2) a; (3) d; (4) b; (5) d; (6) d

Income Property: (1) c; (2) b; (3) c; (4) b; (5) a; (6) b

Fill-In
(1) negative cash flow; (2) sweat equity; (3) compound interest; (4) creditor; (5) amortization; (6) maturity; (7) cash flow; (8) instrument; (9) simple interest; (10) principal

True or False
(1) F; (2) F; (3) T; (4) F; (5) T; (6) T; (7) T; (8) F; (9) T; (10) T

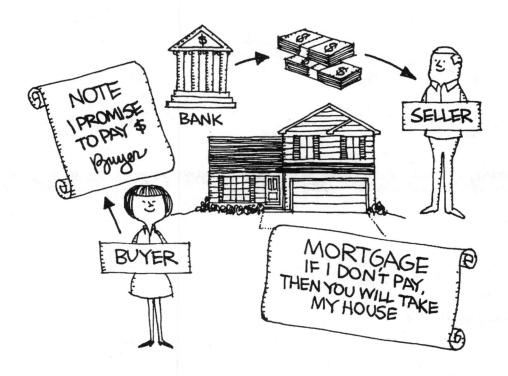

A mortgage involves two separate documents, which is often the cause of a little confusion. One document is the promissory note, or just "note." The other is the mortgage document itself. As mentioned in a previous chapter, the note is the borrower's promise to pay back borrowed money. The mortgage, on the other hand, is the evidence of the collateral, that is, evidence that a property or properties are being used as collateral (or "security") for the loan. If the borrower fails to repay the loan according to the terms of the note, the property may be sold off to pay the debt. This chapter presents and reviews key terms related to notes and mortgages.

Do You Know These Terms?

acceleration clause	mortgagor
alienation clause	novation
assumption	obligee
beneficiary	obligor
condemnation clause	partial release
deed of trust	pledging
default	principal
defeasance	principal balance
delinquent	promissory note
equity of redemption	reconveyance
first mortgage	second mortgage
foreclosure	senior mortgage
hypothecation	subject to
junior mortgage	subordination
mortgage	trustee
mortgage covenants	trustor
mortgagee	

1. Promissory Notes

promissory note	default
obligee	delinquent
obligor	acceleration clause
principal	alienation clause
principal balance	

promissory note

(see also *note* in Chapter 11) an agreement or contract between a lender and a borrower that states (a) the amount of the loan; (b) the terms for repayment of the loan; and (c) the rate of interest that applies to the loan. Promissory notes also show the location and date. Both borrower and lender sign them.

obligee/obligor

The party to a promissory note who is the borrower of the money (or goods or services) is called the *obligor*. The party who is lending the money is called the *obligee*. (One way to remember this is to think of the words obligation and debt. Then you can remember that an "obligor" is a "debtor," i.e., the borrower.)

principal, principal balance

Recall from Chapter 11 that the principal is the amount borrowed. Take care to be clear that the amount still owed on a note after some of the debt has been paid is the *principal balance*, that is, the balance due. Sometimes the principal balance is called the *unpaid principal*, to distinguish it from the *original principal*.

Using Real Estate Terms

Promissory Note

Riverside, California   January 17, 20XX

I promise to pay Riverside Home Mortgage Company   (Obligee) | **Obligee**

located at   4092 Eighth Street, Riverside, California   ,

the sum of   One hundred twenty three thousand and no/100 -

---- dollars, on unpaid principal in installments of twelve hundred

and no/100 ----- dollars on the   first   day of each month

beginning   March 1, 20xx   , continuing until said principal

and interest have been paid.

THIS NOTE may be prepaid in whole or in part at any time without penalty.

IF DEFAULT is made in payment of any installment when due, the entire

principal balance plus accrued interest shall immediately become due | **Acceleration Clause**

at the option of Riverside Home Mortgage Company.

THIS NOTE is secured by a mortgage made in favor of Riverside Home

Mortgage Company and bearing the same date as this note.

Bartholomew Bradshaw
Borrower (Obligor) | **Obligor**

---

default

an unexcused failure to perform a contract obligation, such as
failure to make a payment on a loan at the specified time or within
a specified period.

delinquent

late in the performance of an obligation, such as a loan payment.

Using Real Estate Terms

Charles Sawyer borrowed money for the purchase of his home from Whittaker Mortgage Co. The promissory note that Charles signed contained the following statement:

... There shall be a ten-day grace period for each monthly payment. A $60.00 late charge will be added to any payment made after its grace period.

In June, Charles' payment was four days late. This was within the grace period, so Charles did not have to pay a late fee. In July, however, Charles' payment was 12 days late, and he had to pay an extra $60. His payment was delinquent. ▲▲▲

---

acceleration clause

a provision giving the obligee (lender) the right to demand that the entire balance of the loan be repaid immediately in the event of default. In other words, if the borrower fails to make payments on the note, the lender can demand payment of the full amount. If the borrower cannot pay off the loan, the lender can take the collateral (the house).

Using Real Estate Terms

The promissory note that Charles signed contained the following statement, which is known as an acceleration clause:

...If default is made in payment of any installment when due, the entire principal balance plus accrued interest shall immediately become due at the option of Whittaker Mortgage Co.

When Charles failed to make the payments on the loan for several months, Whittaker Mortgage Co. notified Charles that the total loan was immediately due. Whittaker was exercising the option that was specified in the acceleration clause—it was demanding accelerated payment of the note. ▲▲▲

---

alienation clause

a clause in a note (or a mortgage) giving the lender the right to demand the balance of the loan in the event that the property being used as collateral is sold or otherwise conveyed.

Using Real Estate Terms

Here is an example of an alienation clause:

If the borrower (obligor or mortgagor) sells or otherwise conveys title to the subject property, the lender (Obligee or Mortgagee) may declare the entire unpaid balance immediately due and payable.

Elliot and Mary Baker signed a promissory note for the loan of money to buy their house in Cove Town. A year later they sold the house. At that time, they still owed $79,400 (principal balance) on the loan. When they sold the house, Cove Town Loan Company declared the entire $79,400 due and payable. Cove Town Loan Company did this in accordance with the alienation clause of the promissory note. ▲▲▲

Use the Right Term

Circle the letter of the choice that best completes each statement. Use the definitions of the terms and your logic to determine the best answer. The answers are shown at the end of the chapter.

1. Someone who borrows money and signs a note promising to repay that money _____.

   (a) is the obligee

   (b) is the obligor

   (c) is the promissory

   (d) all of the above

2. A promissory note is a loan contract that _____.

   (a) spells out the terms of the loan

   (b) specifies the amount of the loan

   (c) specifies the interest rate of the loan

   (d) all of the above

3. If exercised (activated), an acceleration clause _____.

   (a) accelerates the repayment of a loan to the lender

   (b) accelerates the delivery of the borrowed money to the borrower

   (c) accelerates the default of the loan

   (d) none of these

4. John failed to make required payments on his loan. He
   _____.

   (a) accelerated

   (b) defaulted

   (c) obligated

   (d) none of the above

5. Paula Douglas signed a promissory note for $98,650. This amount is
   called the _____.

   (a) acceleration amount

   (b) promissory payment amount

   (c) obligee amount

   (d) principal

6. A clause that gives a lender the right to declare the principal balance
   immediately due and payable if a borrower defaults on the note is
   called a/an _____.

   (a) acceleration clause

   (b) alienation clause

   (c) obligee clause

   (d) principal clause

2. Mortgages

mortgage	condemnation clause
mortgagee/mortgagor	hypothecation
mortgage covenants	pledging

mortgage

Like a promissory note, a *mortgage* is an agreement. Although the
two terms are used almost interchangeably in everyday language,
they are not the same. The promissory note (see previous section)
is a promise to repay a loan; it is evidence of a debt. A mortgage,
on the other hand, is evidence of the collateral (the property) for
the loan, and gives the lender the power to take possession of and
sell the property if the borrowed funds are not repaid. In other

words, a mortgage is the document that names the property as security for the loan.

mortgagee, mortgagor

The *mortgagee* is the lender, the party receiving the mortgage. The borrower, or the party receiving the loan, is the *mortgagor*.

mortgage covenants

promises that the borrower makes to the mortgagee regarding the mortgaged property. Commonly, these include a promise to pay the taxes, to carry adequate insurance, to avoid removal or demolishing of the building(s), and to keep the property in good repair. (A covenant is a promise.)

Mortgage covenants are important to the lender mainly for two reasons:

(1) Since the lender carries the risk of a possible default by the borrower, the lender wants to be sure that the property is in good condition. If the lender must foreclose on the property and sell it, he will want the maximum value possible.

(2) The lender does not want any other entity, such as the government, to have a higher claim to the property than his own. If the borrower did not pay the property taxes, for example, they become a lien on the property (and the government, by virtue of this lien, would have a higher or superior claim to the property than the lender).

Items (A) through (D) in the sample mortgage that follows are mortgage covenants.

condemnation clause

a clause stating that if all or part of a property is taken by action of eminent domain (condemnation), any money forthcoming from the condemnation action must go toward payment on the note.

Using Real Estate Terms

ASA Home Loan Company holds the mortgage on Jean Arpino's house. After Jean had purchased the home, the state approved construction of a new highway access road that would cut right through Jean's house. Through an action of eminent domain, more commonly called condemnation, the state took Jean's property and paid what it considered a fair amount for it. The money that the state paid for the property first went to pay off Jean's mortgage, and the remainder went to Jean. The payment to the lender took priority because of the condemnation clause in the mortgage. ▲▲▲

---

hypothecation

> the right of a borrower to possess and use a property while it is serving as collateral.

Using Real Estate Terms

When Carl Segar purchased the little house at the end of Birch Tree Lane, he didn't have enough money to pay cash for it. So he made a cash down payment and took a mortgage for the rest. The mortgagee (lender) was ENT Mortgage Company. As with most mortgages, the property itself was the collateral for the loan. Even though he had mortgaged the property, Carl had the right to possess and use the property, that is, to live in it. This right is known as hypothecation. ▲▲▲

---

pledging

> to give up possession of a property to the lender while it serves as collateral. Pledging is more common in personal property than in real estate. A pawnshop, for example, loans money on property that it holds until the loan is repaid.

Mortgage

This mortgage is made this _____17th_____ day of _____January, 20XX_____,

between _____Bartholomew Bradshaw_____ hereinafter called the Mortgagor, and

Riverside Home Mortgage Company_____ located at_____4092 Eighth Street,

Riverside, California_____, hereinafter called the Mortgagee.

WHEREAS the Mortgagor is indebted to the Mortgagee in the principal sum of

_____one hundred twenty three thousand and no/100_____ dollars, payable

in installments of_____twelve hundred and no/100 ----- dollars including ___8

percent interest_____ on the _____first___ day of each month beginning _____March

1, 20xx_____, continuing until said principal and interest have been paid, as evidenced

by the Mortgagor's note of this same date, hereinafter called the Note.

TO SECURE the Mortgagee the repayment of the indebtedness evidenced by said Note,

with interest thereon, the Mortgagor does hereby mortgage, grant, and convey to the

Mortgagee the following described property in the county of

_____Riverside_____, State of_____California_____.

[Legal description of property inserted here.]

FURTHERMORE, the Mortgagor fully warrants the title to said property and will defend

the same against the lawful claims of all persons.

IF THE MORTGAGOR, his heirs, legal representatives, or assigns pay unto the

Mortgagee, his legal representatives or assigns, all sums due by said Note, then this

mortgage and the estate created hereby shall cease and be null and void.

Sample Mortgage, Continued ...

UNTIL SAID NOTE is fully paid:

> Items (A)
> through (D) are
> covenants.

(A) The Mortgagor agrees to pay all taxes on said land.

(B) The Mortgagor agrees not to remove or demolish buildings or other improvements on the mortgaged land without the approval of the lender.

(C) The Mortgagor agrees to carry adequate insurance to protect the lender in the event of damage or destruction of the mortgaged property.

(D) The Mortgagor agrees to keep the mortgaged property in good repair and not permit waste or deterioration.

IT IS FURTHER AGREED THAT:

> Item (F) is an
> acceleration
> clause.

> Item (G) is an
> alienation
> clause.

> Item (H) is a
> condemnation
> clause.

(E) The Mortgagee shall have the right to inspect the mortgaged property as may be necessary for the security of the Note.

(F) If the Mortgagor does not abide by this mortgage or the accompanying Note, the Mortgagee may declare the entire unpaid balance on the Note immediately due and payable.

(G) If the Mortgagor sells or otherwise conveys title to the mortgaged property, the Mortgagee may declare the entire unpaid balance on the Note immediately due and payable.

(H) If all or part of the mortgaged property is taken by action of eminent domain, any sums of money received shall be applied to the Note.

IN WITNESS WHEREOF, the Mortgagor has executed this mortgage.

Use the Right Term

Circle the letter of the choice that best completes each statement. Use the definitions of the terms and your logic to determine the best answer. The answers are shown at the end of the chapter.

1. A mortgage _____.

   (a) is a note

   (b) is a loan

   (c) names a property as a collateral for a loan

   (d) is illegal

2. The right of a borrower to possess and use a property while it is serving as collateral is called _____.

   (a) tenancy

   (b) pledging

   (c) hypothecation

   (d) hypocation

3. A mortgagor's promise to carry adequate insurance on a property is an example of _____.

   (a) a covenant

   (b) a note

   (c) a premium

   (d) a condemnation clause

4. A document that gives the lender the power to take possession of and sell the property if the borrowed funds are not repaid is _____.

   (a) a forgery

   (b) a rider

   (c) a covenant

   (d) a mortgage

5. A mortgagor's promise to carry adequate insurance on a property is an example of _____.

   (a) a covenant

(b) a note

(c) a premium

(d) a condemnation clause

3. Order of Mortgages

first mortgage   junior mortgage
second mortgage   subordination
senior mortgage

first mortgage

> the mortgage loan with the highest priority for repayment in the event of foreclosure.

second mortgage

> the mortgage loan with the second highest priority for repayment in the event of foreclosure.

Using Real Estate Terms

Mickey and Jane Bloxom borrowed $137,500 from ABC Home Loans to buy their house in Glen River. The mortgage with ABC Home Loans is the first mortgage on the property. Two years later, they needed some additional money, which they borrowed from Jane's Aunt Alice. As security for the loan, Mickey and Jane agreed to give Aunt Alice a second or second mortgage on the house. This means that if the house is sold by foreclosure or any other reason, the money from the sale will first go to ABC Home Loans to pay the first mortgage and after that loan is paid, money from the sale will go to Aunt Alice. ▲▲▲

---

senior mortgage

> a mortgage loan with the highest priority for repayment in the event of foreclosure; a first mortgage.

junior mortgage

> a mortgage loan with a priority lower than the first mortgage. When a first mortgage is paid off, the junior mortgages move up in priority.

subordination

> the voluntary acceptance of a lower-priority position than the mortgagee would ordinarily be entitled to. Subordination may

seem counter-intuitive, but proves useful under certain conditions. For example, a landowner might subordinate his or her position to encourage a developer to buy the land.

Use the Right Term

Circle the letter of the choice that best completes each statement. Use the definitions of the terms and your logic to determine the best answer. The answers are shown at the end of the chapter.

1. Mike Edwards holds a "second" on June Smith's farm. This means that if June Smith sells the property, _____.

   (a) Mike will definitely be paid

   (b) Mike will not get paid

   (c) Mike will get paid if there is money left over after the first mortgage is satisfied

   (d) Mike owns part of June's house

2. A senior mortgage _____.

   (a) is a first mortgage

   (b) is either a first or a second mortgage

   (c) is not a first mortgage

   (d) none of the above

3. A second mortgage _____.

   (a) is not as safe an investment as a first mortgage

   (b) is a junior mortgage

   (c) is not a senior mortgage

   (d) all of the above

4. The voluntary permitting of one's priority of position with a mortgage to be lowered is called _____.

   (a) a second mortgage

   (b) a senior mortgage

   (c) insubordination

   (d) subordination

4. Endings

defeasance	novation
partial release	foreclosure
subject to	equity of redemption
assumption	

defeasance

the end of a mortgage when the note is paid in full. A defeasance clause in a mortgage will have language to the effect that the "mortgage and the estate created hereby shall cease and be null and void when the note is paid in full."

partial release

release of a portion of a mortgaged property from the mortgage after part of the loan has been repaid.

Using Real Estate Terms

Sam Morris purchased 500 acres of good farmland, which he mortgaged for $990,000 with a note to the seller. Since he planned to give his daughter 50 acres free and clear, he asked that the seller release 50 acres free and clear of mortgage encumbrance as soon as he had paid $100,000 against the principal. This example release was a partial release. ▲▲▲

---

subject to

the change of the primary debtor on a loan from the seller of the property to the buyer of the property by means of a clause in the purchase agreement, in which the buyer states awareness of the existing loan and offers to buy the property *subject to* the existing loan. In this case, the buyer makes the loan payments, but the seller is still the responsible party. If the buyer fails to make the payments, the lender will look to the seller for payment.

assumption

the change of the primary debtor on a loan from the seller of the property to the buyer of the property. The buyer agrees in writing to be personally liable for the terms and conditions of the existing mortgage on the property. The seller continues to be liable, and if the buyer defaults on the loan, the lender can look to the original mortgagor, i.e., the seller, for payment. In some cases, the lender will release the seller from liability, which is done by a *novation*.

novation

> the substitution of a new contract, debt, or obligation for a previous or existing contract, debt, or obligation between the same or different parties. There are three different types of novation in the context of real estate loans: (a) the debtor and creditor remain the same, but a new debt replaces the old; (b) the creditor and the debt remain the same, but a new debtor is substituted; (c) the debtor and the debt remain the same, but the creditor is replaced by another. The requirements for a novation are a valid original contract, an agreement by all parties to extinguish the previous obligation, the extinguishments of the old contract, and the validity of the new contract.

Using Real Estate Terms

When Gloria George bought Jim Ramsey's house, the lender and the debt remained the same, but Gloria was substituted as the borrower. This arrangement is an example of novation. Afterward, the lender looked to Gloria for repayment of the loan, not to Jim. ▲▲▲

---

foreclosure

> the sale of a property to satisfy an unpaid debt.

Using Real Estate Terms

When Norman and Olivia could not make the loan payments on their house, the lender foreclosed on the property. ▲▲▲

---

equity of redemption

> a property owner's right or privilege to redeem a property prior to the final moment of foreclosure.

Using Real Estate Terms

When the lender foreclosed on Norman and Olivia's house, the property was scheduled to be sold at a public auction. Before the sale, however, Norman and Olivia inherited a large sum of money from a relative. They decided to use the inheritance to redeem their house from foreclosure, which they were able to do legally according to equity of redemption privilege. ▲▲▲

Use the Right Term

Circle the letter of the choice that best completes each statement. Use the definitions of the terms and your logic to determine the best answer. The answers are shown at the end of the chapter.

1. When Nancy Trower paid off the loan on her property, her mortgage became null and void. This is an example of

   _____.

   (a) defeasance

   (b) novation

   (c) partial release

   (d) malfeasance

2. When Adam Smith failed to make the payments on his note, the mortgagor sold Adam's property. This is an example of

   _____.

   (a) novation

   (b) full release

   (c) foreclosure

   (d) illegal seizure

3. According to the principle of _____, if Adam had obtained sufficient money before the mortgagee sold it, he could redeem his property.

   (a) fairness

   (b) equity of redemption

   (c) repurchase money

   (d) none of the above

4. In which of the following processes does a seller have the least liability for the existing loan?

   (a) subject to

   (b) assumption

   (c) novation

   (d) equity of redemption

5. Deeds of Trust

deed of trust	trustor
beneficiary	reconveyance
trustee	

In some circumstances and/or in some states, a deed of trust or other security agreement is used instead of a mortgage. Three possibilities include *deed of trust* or *trust deed*, *equitable mortgage*, and *security deed*.

deed of trust

a three-party agreement to secure a debt. Also called a *trust deed*, the parties to this type of contract are a borrower (trustor), lender (beneficiary), and a neutral third party (trustee). According to a trust deed, the borrower executes a deed to the neutral third party rather than to the lender. When the debt (promissory note) has been paid, the lender has the trustee reconvey the title back to the borrower. If the trustor defaults on the loan, however, the lender has the trustee sell the property to pay off the loan.

beneficiary

in a deed of trust, the beneficiary is the lender. Note that a deed of trust is set up for the benefit of (to protect) the lender.

trustee

a neutral third party that holds the property (title or deed) in trust for another party or parties.

trustor

the creator of a trust. In a deed of trust, the trustor is the borrower.

reconveyance

the return of title to a property to the trustor (borrower) upon payment in full of the note. The document used for this purpose is called a *reconveyance* or *release deed*.

Using Real Estate Terms

Carl Jones signed a promissory note for $162,000 from Terracina Mortgage Company. He signed a deed of trust making Riverbed Title and Trust Company the trustee. This means that Riverbed Title and Trust Company is holding the title to the property until Carl pays off the note with Terracina Mortgage. Then Terracina Mortgage will tell Riverbed Title and Trust to reconvey title of the property back to Carl. See the terms of the deed of trust agreement in the following example. ▲▲▲

Deed of Trust

This Deed of Trust, made this _____19th_____ day of _____May, 20XX_____,

between _____Carl Jones_____, hereinafter called the Trustor, and ___Terracina Mortgage___

__Company__ located at ___4042 Terracina, Riverbed, Colorado___, hereinafter

called the Trustor, and _____Riverbed Title and Trust Company_____, hereinafter

called the Trustee.

WITNESSETH: To secure repayment of a Promissory Note in the principal sum of

___one hundred sixty two thousand and no/100___ dollars of this same date,

hereinafter called the Note, and to secure agreements as listed below, the Trustor irrevocably

grants and conveys to the Trustee, in trust with power of sale, the following described

property in the county of ___Riverbed___, State of _____Colorado_____.

[Legal description of property inserted here.]

FURTHERMORE, the Trustor fully warrants the title to said property and will defend the

same against the lawful claims of all persons.

UPON WRITTEN REQUEST by the Beneficiary to the Trustee stating that all sums secured

hereby have been paid, and upon surrender of this Deed and said Note to the Trustee for

cancellation, the Trustee shall reconvey the above described property to the Trustor.

THIS DEED BINDS all parties hereto, their successors, assigns, heirs, devises,

administrators, and executors.

UNTIL SAID NOTE IS PAID IN FULL:

Covenants

(A) The Trustor will pay all taxes on said property.

(B) The Trustor will not remove or demolish any buildings or other improvements on
said property without the express approval of the Beneficiary.

(C) The Trustor will carry adequate insurance to protect the Beneficiary in the event
of damage or destruction of said property.

(D) The Trustor will keep said property in good repair and will not permit waste or
deterioration.

(E) The Beneficiary shall have the right to inspect the property as may be necessary
for the security of the note.

Condemnation
Clause

(F) If all or part of said property is taken by eminent domain, any money received
shall be applied to the Note.

(continued ...)

Sample Deed of Trust, Continued.

UPON DEFAULT BY THE TRUSTOR in payment of the debt secured hereby, or the nonperformance of any agreement hereby made, the Beneficiary:

    (G) May declare all sums secured hereby immediately due and payable.

    (H) May enter and take possession of said property and collect the rents and profits thereof.

    (I) May demand the Trustee sell said property in accordance with state law, apply the proceeds to the unpaid portion of the Note, and deliver to the purchaser a Trustee's Deed conveying Title to said property.

THE TRUSTEE ACCEPTS THIS TRUST when this Deed, properly executed and acknowledged, is made a public record. The Beneficiary may substitute a successor to the Trustee named herein by recording such change in the public records of the county where said property is located.

    Trustor

Use the Right Term

Circle the letter of the choice that best completes each statement. Use the definitions of the terms and your logic to determine the best answer. The answers are shown at the end of the chapter.

1. In the deed of trust example above, _____ will pay taxes on the property.

    (a) the trustee

    (b) the trustor

    (c) the seller

    (d) the beneficiary

2. In the deed of trust example above, Carl Jones is the _____.

    (a) trustor

    (b) trustee

    (c) beneficiary

    (d) none of these

3. The trustor in a deed of trust _____.

   (a) is also the beneficiary because he or she eventually benefits by receiving the title to the property

   (b) is also the borrower or obligor on the note

   (c) is also the seller of the property

   (d) none of these

4. In a deed of trust, the lender is the beneficiary because _____.

   (a) he or she benefits from the interest paid on the note

   (b) he or she benefits from fees paid by the trustee

   (c) he or she is benefiting from the protection provided by having a third party hold the title

   (d) the lender is not the beneficiary

Review & Practice: Notes and Mortgages

acceleration clause	hypothecation
alienation clause	novation
defeasance clause	obligor
default	reconveyance
first mortgage	trustee

Select the term from the list above that best fits the blank in each sentence below.

1. A/An _____ is a provision giving the obligee (lender) the right to demand that the entire balance of the loan be repaid immediately in the event of default.

2. The party to a promissory note who is the borrower of the money (or goods or services) is called the _____.

3. The right of a borrower to possess and use a property while it is serving as collateral is called _____.

4. The mortgage loan with the highest priority for repayment in the event of foreclosure is _____.

5. *Mortgage and the estate created hereby shall cease and be null and void when the note is paid in full.* This is an example of a/an _____.

6. *If the borrower (obligor or mortgagor) sells or otherwise conveys title to the subject property, the lender (Obligee or Mortgagee) may declare the entire unpaid balance immediately due and payable.* This is an example of a/an _____.

7. The substitution of a new contract, debt, or obligation for a previous or existing contract, debt, or obligation between the same or different parties is _____.

8. The neutral third party that holds the property (title or deed) in trust for another party or parties is called the _____.

9. A/an _____ refers to the return of title to a property to the trustor (borrower) upon payment in full of the note.

10. A/an _____ is an unexcused failure to perform a contract obligation.

Short Answer

Use the space provided to answer the following questions.

1. List the three main elements of a *promissory note* (besides the location and date of the agreement and signatures of borrower and lender).

2. What is the purpose of an *acceleration clause*? Who does it protect?

3. What is the difference between an *acceleration clause* and an *alienation clause*?

4. List four common *mortgage covenants*.

5. George Parker's property is right in the path of a new county road. The county takes the property by its right of eminent domain (see Chapter 2), and pays what it deems a fair amount. George's mortgage contains a condemnation clause. What happens to the money that the county pays for the property?

6. Explain the difference between a *first mortgage* and a *second mortgage*.

7. Give the definitions for *defeasance* and *reconveyance*.

8. What is *equity of redemption*? When is it used?

9. What is *partial release*? Give an example.

10. Complete the following table by indicating who makes the payments, who is responsible (liable) for the loan, and what document is used to make the agreement. Use each term as often as needed.

buyer   purchase agreement
seller   separate written agreement
new note

	makes payments	responsible party	document
subject to			
assumption			
novation			

True or False

Indicate whether each of the following statements is true or false by circling T or F. The answers are shown at the end of the chapter.

T F 1. A deed of trust is an agreement or contract among three parties: a buyer, a seller, and a beneficiary.

T F 2. In a trust deed arrangement, the trustor is the buyer of the property.

T F   3. The trustee is the person or entity who is entrusted with the title to a property until all the payments are made.

T F   4. An alienation clause protects the lender in the event that a borrower sells the house that is being used as security.

T F   5. Default refers to the "boilerplate" language in contracts. If no special language is needed, the parties use the default language.

T F   6. In a deed of trust agreement, when the loan has been paid in full, the beneficiary (lender) tells the trustee (neutral third party) to deliver title to the trustor (borrower).

T F   7. The two parts of a mortgage are the mortgage document and the deed of trust.

T F   8. In a deed of trust agreement, the taxes are usually paid by the trustee.

T F   9. The two parts of a mortgage are the note and the mortgage document.

T F   10. A covenant is a promise.

Answers

Promissory Notes: (1) b; (2) d; (3) a; (4) b; (5) d; (6) a

Mortgages: (1) c; (2) c; (3) a; (4) d; (5) a

Order of Mortgages: (1) a; (2) c; (3) b; (4) c

Endings: (1) a; (2) c; (3) b; (4) b

Deeds of Trust: (1) b; (2) a; (3) b; (4) c

Fill-In
(1) acceleration clause; (2) obligor; (3) hypothecation; (4) first mortgage; (5) defeasance clause; (6) alienation clause; (7) novation; (8) trustee; (9) reconveyance; (10) default

True or False
(1) T; (2) T; (3) T; (4) T; (5) F; (6) T; (7) F; (8) F; (9) T; (10) T

Appendix I
CHAPTER TERMS

Chapter 1: Describing Land

acre
air lot
assessor's map
base line
bench mark
chattel
contour map
corner lot
cul de sac
fixture
flag lot
front foot

government survey
guide meridian
improvement
inside lot
key lot
lot, block, tract
meridian
metes and bounds
monument
personal property
plat
principal meridian

quadrangle
quarter section
range
raw land
real estate
real property
relief map
section
single-loaded street
standard parallel
T-lot
township

Chapter 2: Land Rights & Interests

air rights
condemnation
dominant tenement
easement
easement appurtenant
easement by necessity
easement in gross
eminent domain
encroachment
encumbrance
escheat
estate
estate at will
estate for years
fee simple absolute
freehold estate

general lien
inverse condemnation
involuntary lien
judgment lien
lease
leasehold estate
leasehold interest
lessee/lessor
lien
life estate
life estate pur autre vie
life tenant
littoral rights
mechanic's lien
mortgage
mortgage lien

periodic tenancy
property tax lien
quiet enjoyment
remainder interest
remainderman
reversionary interest
reversioner
right of way
riparian rights
servient tenement
specific lien
tenancy at
sufferance
voluntary lien

Chapter 3: Ownership

community property
concurrent ownership
estate in severalty
joint tenancy
partition
right of survivorship

separate property
sole ownership
tenancy by the entirety
tenancy for life; life estate,
tenancy in common
undivided interest

unities
unity of interest
unity of possession
unity of time
unity of title

Chapter 4: Transfer of Ownership

accession	decedent	intestate
accretion	dedication	land patent
administrator/administratrix	deed	legacy, legatee
adverse possession	devise, devisee	nuncupative (oral) will
alienation of title	executor/executrix	probate
alluvion	executor's deed	quitclaim deed
avulsion	forfeiture of title	reliction
bargain and sale deed	gift deed	Statute of Frauds
bequeath, bequest	grant	testate
codicil	grant deed	testator, testatrix
consideration	grantee	warranty deed
convey, conveyance	grantor	will
correction deed	guardian deed	
covenants and warranties,	holographic will	

Chapter 5: Public Records and Title Insurance

abstract of title	lender's policy	record
actual notice	lis pendens index	title cloud
chain of title	marketable title	title insurance
color of title	notary public	title report
constructive notice	opinion of title	title search
defect on title	owner's policy	Torrens system
grantor/grantee index	public recorder's office	tract index
inquiry notice	quiet title suit	unrecorded interest

Chapter 6: Purchase Agreements

acceptance	home inspection	purchase agreement
as is	instrument	purchase contract
brokerage commission	latent defects	purchase offer
buyer default	liquidated damages	purchase price
close of escrow; closing date	loan commitment letter	rider (addendum,
contingency	notification	attachment)
counteroffer	offer to purchase	roof inspection
damages	perform	sales contract
default	pest control inspection;	specific performance
deposit receipt	termite inspection	time is of the essence
disclosure statement	possession	time limits
dry rot	property description	
earnest money deposit	prorating	

Chapter 7: Exchanges and Other Agreements

bill of sale	contract for deed	exercise an option
binder	delayed exchange	installment contract
conditional sales contract	equitable title	land contract

lease-option
letter of intent
option fee
optionee

optionor
qualified intermediary
right of first refusal
tax-deferred exchange

trading up
vendee
vendor

Chapter 8: Escrow

beneficiary statement
close into escrow
closing costs
closing date
closing meeting
closing statement
concurrent recording

dry closing
escrow
escrow agent
escrow closing
escrow fees
escrow instructions
escrow officer

good faith estimate
outside of escrow
prorating
RESPA
settlement statement
walk-through

Chapter 9: Appraisal

adjusted market price
adjustments
appraisal
appraisal approaches
buyers' market
capitalize
CMA
comparables
correlation
cost approach
curable depreciation
depreciation
economic
obsolescence

effective gross income
FIRREA
functional
obsolescence
gross rent multiplier
highest and best use
income approach
incurable depreciation
market approach;
    value approach
market value
net operating income
operating expenses
physical deterioration

projected gross income
reconciliation
replacement cost
reproduction cost
scheduled gross
income
sellers' market
square-foot method
subject property
USPAP
vacancy allowance
valuation

Chapter 10: Leases

actual eviction
assignee
assignment
assignor
constructive eviction
contract rent
economic rent
escalator clause
estate at will
estate for years
eviction
graduated rent

gross lease
ground lease
ground rent
holdover tenant
index lease
leasehold estate
lessee
lessor
month-to-month lease
net lease; triple net
    lease
option clause

participation clause
percentage lease
periodic estate
quiet enjoyment
retaliatory eviction
reversion
step-up rent
sublease
sublessee
sublessor
sublet

Chapter 11: Finance

amortization	depreciation	note
amortization table	equity	principal
annual percentage rate	gross income	rate
(APR)	instrument	simple interest
appreciation	interest	sweat equity
borrower	maturity	term
cash flow	negative cash flow	usury
compound interest	net income	
creditor	net profit	

Chapter 12: Notes and Mortgages

acceleration clause	foreclosure	pledging
alienation clause	hypothecation	principal
assumption	junior mortgage	principal balance
beneficiary	mortgage	promissory note
condemnation clause	mortgage covenants	reconveyance
deed of trust	mortgagee	second mortgage
default	mortgagor	senior mortgage
defeasance	novation	subject to
delinquent	obligee	subordination
equity of redemption	obligor	trustee
first mortgage	partial release	trustor

Appendix II
INDEX OF TERMS

About the Author

Learning the Language of Real Estate helps readers learn new concepts and master the language that goes with them. Both of these areas are long familiar to author Barbara Cox, Ph.D., who brings academic training and professional experience to the writing of this book. Dr. Cox earned her doctorate in education and psychology at Stanford University, where she studied and conducted research on cognitive development and language acquisition. In these areas, she has authored or co-authored 70 books as well as numerous articles and reports. Her understanding of the need to link the learning of unfamiliar concepts and language to familiar, easily understood situations is clearly seen in these pages. Her professional life includes work as educator and researcher at the college/university level, communications and strategic planning consultant for non-profit organizations, corporate trainer, and textbook author.

The author's experience teaching real estate courses adds the other key dimension to this work—the language of real estate. As Director of Technology for the Orange County Association of Realtors® in California for three years, Dr. Cox established and directed the Technology Education Center. Among the 22 real estate technology courses she developed were DRE-approved Internet Marketing and E-Mail How-To, Real Estate (Agent) Finance, Contact Management, and Basic Computing.

Barbara Cox is an author of the *Dictionary of Real Estate: A Handy Reference Pocket Edition* (South-Western, 2001) with Jerry Cox and David Silver-Westrick. With Wm. Koelzer, she is author of *Web Marketing for the Real Estate Professional* and *Internet Marketing in Real Estate* (South-Western, 2001). Forthcoming works in real estate include the *Comprehensive Dictionary of Real Estate* with Jerry Cox and David Silver-Westrick (South-Western, 2003).